step-by-step
meditation

step-by-step
meditation

gain focus and serenity with
simple-to-follow techniques shown
in more than 250 photographs

DORIEL HALL

LORENZ BOOKS

To the voice of Love within each of us that waits to be heard in meditation and expressed in our daily lives.

This edition is published by Lorenz Books, an imprint of Anness Publishing Ltd, Blaby Road, Wigston, Leicestershire LE18 4SE; info@anness.com

www.lorenzbooks.com; www.annesspublishing.com

If you like the images in this book and would like to investigate using them for publishing, promotions or advertising, please visit our website www.practicalpictures.com for more information.

Publisher: Joanna Lorenz
Managing Editor: Helen Sudell
Project Editor: Ann Kay
Text Editor: Beverley Jollands
Designer: Ann Samuel
Special Photography: Michelle Garrett
Photographer's Assistant: Lisa Shalet
Production Controller: Helen Wang

A CIP catalogue record for this book is available from the British Library.

PUBLISHER'S NOTE
The author and publisher disclaim any liability resulting from the techniques and information in this book. If you are concerned about any aspect of your physical or psychological health, always seek professional help. It is advisable to consult a qualified medical professional before undertaking any exercise routines – especially if you have a medical condition or are pregnant.

Contents

Introduction

Meditation is a way of focusing the mind, stilling the endless mental chatter that saps our energy and creates stress and negative feelings. Although it requires us to set time aside to turn our attention inward, the benefits gained in solitude can transform our relationships. The practice of meditation increases our awareness of ourselves and of how we relate to the rest of creation, and enables us to live fully in each moment with contentment, serenity and love.

We live our lives on many levels, in body, mind and spirit, and the techniques that lead us into the meditative state are designed to refresh and harmonize our energies at all levels. Exercises that stretch and relax the body and deepen the breathing relieve tension and stress, allowing the consciousness to awaken. The meditation techniques presented in this book follow the principles set out by the Indian sage Patanjali, whose teachings on yoga as the path to meditation still form the basis of most of the yoga taught today.

When the mind is freed from the turmoil of everyday concerns it is able to turn inward to find spiritual wisdom in a state of expanded awareness. Reflecting on what we have learned, we can use the insight we gain to transform our daily lives, expressing who we really are and bringing about what we feel we are here to achieve.

There are many routes to the meditative state: it can be reached in stillness or movement, with sound or in silence. Any ordinary activity that is performed with complete concentration and mindfulness can become a form of meditation. Meditation is both the means and the end: the practice and transformation of consciousness that is its result. This book explores how to make it a natural part of daily life, as essential as sleeping and eating.

What is Meditation?

During an experience of meditation we are calm, aware, focused, happy and loving. We let go of the burden of ourselves and enter into a wider state of consciousness. Having achieved this wonderful state, we can then learn to transfer these same attitudes to all our interactions and to maintain them in everyday situations, regardless of what is happening around us. It is possible, through the regular practice of meditation, to transform the quality of our lives totally, living each moment untroubled by negativity and the stress that it inevitably builds up.

Finding your inner self

Human beings have many levels: our physical bodies, energy flow, instinctive responses, thinking processes and wisdom each play a vital part in our overall functioning, and all need to be in balance to ensure health and wellbeing. All too often, however, a hectic modern lifestyle can unbalance these levels, making us feel jaded in body, mind and spirit. The regular practice of meditation helps us to rebalance ourselves so that all the levels are able to work together in harmony.

Meditation has three aspects: the regular practice of techniques that enable us to reach the meditative state, the experience of the state of meditation, and recreating this state in daily life. There are traditional meditation techniques appropriate to all temperaments and levels of attainment. They all involve symbolically "going up into the solitude of the mountains" so that we can then "return to the bustle of the marketplace" and live a changed life as a result of our experience.

We practise meditation because we believe (with Robert Browning) that:

> There is an inmost centre in us all,
> Where Truth abides in fullness…and to know
> Rather consists in opening out a way
> Whence the imprisoned splendour may escape.

Meditation allows us to experience that splendour for ourselves and live our lives in the glow of our own inner radiance.

"Only the present moment exists."
Traditional wisdom

removing inner obstructions

The path to and from our "inmost centre" may be obstructed by lack of awareness, self-obsession, the stress of an unbalanced lifestyle, or by negative attitudes and thought patterns.

Most of us try to crowd too much activity into our lives, and lack the stillness and silence that are necessary to rebalance the nervous system. Regular meditation

△ Traditional meditation is practised with the spine erect and the body motionless. The mind is still but alert, vibrant and focused inward.

practice establishes a healthy rhythm of activity and rest for both mind and body. Our minds are constantly active, mulling over current problems, planning anxiously for a future we cannot control, regretting past actions or creating personal doctrines

△ **Symbolically compared with the solitude of the mountains, meditation involves a withdrawal from the bustle of human activity.**

▷ **These traditional clay figures in a circle of friendship represent the unity nurtured by the meditative way of life.**

and dogmas, opinions and prejudices. These mental "games" draw us, like magnets, away from the present moment. Meditation teaches us to live in the moment, and grow through the experiences of here and now. When we are inclined to wallow in negative emotions such as anger or resentment, and to see insults and dangers where none exist, meditation helps us to replace defensive energy-sapping reactions with open and trusting responses that enable us to build loving relationships.

reducing stress

If you practise the meditation techniques outlined in this book regularly and with enthusiasm, you will soon start to feel the benefits, as both the causes and the effects of stress diminish.

Stress is a normal part of life, and a certain amount is essential to motivate and develop humans, but the pace and complexity of life in modern Western society can overburden our systems and block our natural ability to manage stress. Human beings are (as far as we know) the only animals with brains that are constantly

thinking – but the result may be that we allow ourselves to remain stuck in negative thought patterns, squandering our precious energy and unbalancing the nervous system.

Like that of any other animal, the human nervous system operates instinctively and is programmed to deal physically with threats to survival. Stress is a natural reaction that enables us to respond to danger, either by fighting or running away. Once the threatening episode is over the nervous system should rebalance itself as we return peacefully to our normal activities. Unlike other animals, however, humans are apt to remain in a state of arousal, because we go on feeling anxious about past and future events, as well as preferring to be continually active and stimulated in the present.

Because stress hormones make us feel excited, it is easy to become addicted to activities and challenges that trigger their release. This is why we want to watch exciting programmes on television and take part in testing activities. But if we remain in a constant state of arousal, we deny our bodily systems the chance to rest and renew themselves. Stress accumulates until the system reaches breaking point – and the result is illness and malfunctioning of the body or mind. By practising the techniques of meditation, we can reverse this build-up of stress by learning to stop and consciously clear the mind and emotions of negative attitudes the moment we become aware of them.

STRESS AND YOUR HEALTH
Meditation practice can help to reduce the unpleasant effects of prolonged stress, protecting you from symptoms such as:
- muscle tension and pain in the joints
- tension and migraine headaches
- the inability to concentrate or think clearly
- digestive problems, which may include diabetes
- interrupted sleep patterns
- breathing difficulties
- cardiovascular problems
- allergic reactions
- physical fatigue
- nervous exhaustion
- weakness of the immune system
- other auto-immune problems

▽ **Regular meditation gives you the energy and clarity you need to deal with the multiple demands of daily life.**

Treading the path of the ancients

The practice of meditation may be as old as humanity itself, and its origins certainly predate written records. When we look at the most ancient civilizations that still exist today, such as the aborigines of Australia or the native peoples of North and South America, we find that meditation, and spiritual practices generally, have always been the special preserve of those few who were chosen to undergo many years of training and tests before being considered fit to gain access to hidden wisdom and to be the spiritual leaders of their people.

In many cultures, spiritual mastery, and the techniques that led to it, were taught secretly to those destined to become spiritual leaders – either by being chosen at a very young age (like the Dalai Lama of Tibetan Buddhism) or by being born into a family chosen to fulfil this role for generations (such as the Brahmins of Hinduism). It is only recently, with the explosion of worldwide communications, that this secret wisdom has become widely available to all who are prepared to learn and practise the techniques.

△ In the Buddhist tradition, the energy and insight gained from meditation are dedicated to the enlightenment of all living beings.

meditation techniques and traditional lifestyles

When they are stripped of the symbolism and mystery that have traditionally concealed them from prying eyes, the secret meditation techniques of every culture are remarkably similar. These techniques all help the meditator to quieten body and mind and to let go of thoughts about the past, the future and daily life in order to turn attention inward. This switches the nervous system into the "all is well" state of serenity and changes the quality of the brain waves from active to reflective. In these conditions, an experience of the state of meditation can develop.

In many traditions, spiritual practices are learned while the meditator lives in a

▷ The doctrine of love and trust preached by Jesus and other great spiritual leaders stemmed from their experience of the meditative state.

community, such as an ashram or monastery, that is set apart from society as a whole. Regular solitary meditation is always balanced with activity performed as a service to that community. When the meditator is considered able to maintain a state of meditation "in the marketplace" as easily as "on the mountain top", he is sent out to preach and teach the wider community. Once back in the world, there is a danger of spiritual teachers being seduced by fame and the adulation of their followers and falling from grace, becoming "false gurus".

Only a very few are accepted for training. In the past, the majority of people were excluded – especially women (who were the property of their menfolk), serfs, peasants and labourers (who were virtually owned by rich and powerful landlords), and foreigners. Nevertheless, members of these excluded groups have produced some of the greatest practitioners, in spite of the obstacles they have faced. In today's world we are fortunate that almost everyone – regardless of nationality, class or gender – has the opportunity to practise the meditation techniques of the ancient spiritual traditions.

Buddhism and Christianity

The Buddha was a Hindu prince, born in India around 560 BC. He left his life of luxury when he saw the sufferings endured

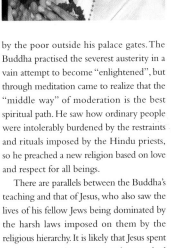

◁ **The Maharishi Mahesh Yogi's Transcendental Meditation was made popular in the West during the 1960s by celebrities such as the Beatles.**

▽ **This 18th-century miniature depicts a holy man seated in Siddhasana, one of the principal postures used in meditation.**

by the poor outside his palace gates. The Buddha practised the severest austerity in a vain attempt to become "enlightened", but through meditation came to realize that the "middle way" of moderation is the best spiritual path. He saw how ordinary people were intolerably burdened by the restraints and rituals imposed by the Hindu priests, so he preached a new religion based on love and respect for all beings.

There are parallels between the Buddha's teaching and that of Jesus, who also saw the lives of his fellow Jews being dominated by the harsh laws imposed on them by the religious hierarchy. It is likely that Jesus spent periods in a meditative state as he preached love and forgiveness. Both the Buddha and Jesus restored basic human freedoms, but after their deaths their followers built new religious institutions in their names that again suppressed this freedom. Today we in the West are again free to choose our own path to the hidden splendour within, despite all the pressures of a greedy and secular world. We should take advantage of this opportunity.

▽ **In North American and other shamanic traditions, rhythmic drumming is a powerful way of connecting with the world of spirit.**

meditation and Hinduism

Hinduism is a vast melting pot of ideas based on the teachings of the Vedic scriptures, which are thought to date from about 2000 BC. Two schools of meditation that are currently popular in the West have arisen out of Hinduism.

The first is that of the Indian sage Patanjali. His *raja yoga* – the "royal path" of meditation – was originally designed for Hindu monks. It teaches yoga posture, breathing and relaxation as preparations for meditation. Many Western yoga and exercise systems are based on these aspects of Patanjali's teaching. Another popular path is Transcendental Meditation (TM), which was introduced to the West by the Indian Maharishi Mahesh Yogi in the early 1960s. His system, which is designed to fit into everyday life, promotes mental relaxation – leading to the state of meditation – through sitting twice daily for silent repetition of a personal *mantra*, or sacred sound, specially chosen for each individual.

Universal meditation techniques

◁ The postures traditionally used for meditation allow the body to stay motionless while keeping the spine erect.

▽ Wrap a shawl or blanket around your shoulders so that you stay comfortably warm while sitting still to meditate.

Most classical meditation techniques are common to all the great spiritual traditions, although their forms may vary. Whatever the methods used, the meditation will follow a similar pattern.

For meditation practice to bear fruit in daily life there are four essential elements: detaching the attention from competing distractions outside and within; returning the mind to a single focus in order to enter a state of expanded awareness (the state of meditation); recalling and reflecting on the insights gained while in the meditative state; learning to apply these insights to daily life. The final stage of mastery is to live constantly in the meditative state, "enlightened while still embodied". It is said that the effects of meditation are cumulative and that "no effort is ever wasted".

stilling the body

Settling into a position that can be held without effort means that the body can cease to occupy our attention. Hindus, Buddhists, Zen Buddhists and yogis usually sit on their heels or cross-legged on the floor. Christians may kneel and many Westerners prefer to sit upright on a firm chair. Classical yoga postures are designed to hold the body upright and still for long periods. The eyes may be closed to avoid outside distractions or open to gaze upon a specific object.

breathing and chanting

Slowing and deepening the breath induces relaxation of the nervous system. Chanting aloud is a traditional way to lengthen each breath and the repetition of a mantra or prayer is soothing and uplifting. Buddhists, Christians, Hindus and yogis all practise chanting and repetition, either aloud or silently. A string of beads – such as the *mala* used by yogis or the Christian rosary – is often used for counting the repetitions of a mantra or prayer.

focusing on a single object

When the attention is focused, the incessant chattering of the mind quietens naturally, and we become oblivious to outer or inner distractions. Sound is a universal focus, and may take the form of music, the note of a Tibetan singing bowl, a mantra or *nada* (the mystical sounds of our inner vibration).

Gazing – often upon a flower or lighted candle – is another universal practice. Christians may choose to focus on a picture of Christ or a saint, Hindus and Buddhists on an image of a divine being or incarnation of God. If you prefer an impersonal image, you might choose the Sanskrit symbol of OM, the *shri yantra* or a *mandala* (both of which are pictorial

◁ You may wish to sit for meditation before a low table holding natural or symbolic objects on which to concentrate your gaze.

▽ One of the most basic focusing techniques involves gazing at a single object: focusing on a flower helps you to feel at one with creation.

representations of universal energies). The focus may be something touched or felt, such as mala beads or the breath within the body. Even the senses of smell and taste may serve as focal points for meditation.

observation and acceptance

"Witnessing impartially" consists of relaxed observation and acceptance of what is, without any reaction of liking, disliking, criticism or judgement. After watching the contents of the mind in this way we can record them truthfully in a diary. Once we stop reacting instinctively we can start to respond from the heart and open ourselves to life as it is. This is the aim of both Western and Eastern psychotherapies.

mental visualization

Visualization is the intentional creation of a mental image or series of images, which may be of objects, feelings or symbols, as a focus for meditation practice. Informal visualizations are often used by Western psychotherapists and might, for instance, involve experiencing a walk by the sea or in the countryside using all five senses. Skill in visualization enhances the ability to create and maintain healthy and happy attitudes, thoughts and emotions, replacing former negative feelings.

healing through love

"Placing the mind in the heart" is an essential step, for love is an attribute of the heart – or feeling nature – and not of the mind. Love should serve our highest aspirations. When loving feelings and thoughts radiate outward from the heart like light from a lighthouse, both the meditator and those meditated upon receive healing.

living in loving kindness

When we live consciously from the highest we can glimpse in meditation, we are living from the heart. We feel strong, relaxed, focused, accepting, creative and joyful.

People in all ages and traditions have achieved this goal. The Hindu tradition has always perceived the divinity in everyone – hence the Indian greeting of "*Namaste*", meaning "The divine in me greets the divine in you". Both Buddhists and yogis practise the meditation of loving kindness, in which love is beamed from the heart to all sentient beings, including those who cause pain and distress. Jesus said, "You shall love the Lord your God with all your heart and soul and mind and strength, and your

neighbour as yourself." St Francis of Assisi included all of nature in his love, and the English monk who wrote *The Cloud of Unknowing* declared that "God can be known by thought never – only by love can he be known." This wisdom is available to us all: we can find it for ourselves through the practice of meditation.

▷ The Buddha is represented in contemplation of a lotus, the symbol of enlightenment, with his right hand raised in a gesture of reassurance.

Patanjali's system

△ This stone seal showing a seated yogi belongs to the Harappa civilization of the Indus Valley, which worshipped a deity associated with meditation in the third millennium BC.

The *Yoga Sutras* of Patanjali is an ancient Indian text on yoga meditation (raja yoga) which forms the basis of most yoga taught today, and of the meditation techniques presented in this book. Western yoga teachers study the text as part of their training, even when the yoga they teach is predominantly *hatha*, or physical, yoga. The core hatha yoga text (*Hatha Yoga Pradipika*) agrees with Patanjali that "Hatha yoga is to be practised solely for the purpose of attaining raja yoga" – in other words, as a preparation for meditation. All the benefits of yoga for health and stress relief are incidental to its main purpose, which is "the settling of the mind into silence" to achieve the state of meditation.

who was Patanjali?

Yoga did not originate with Patanjali and he may not even have been a single person. All that is known about him is that he fused together the many yogic traditions that existed in his time – thought to be around 100 BC to AD 100 – into one coherent philosophical system. Some scholars consider that the section on the "eight limbs"of yoga (which includes the hatha yoga element) was added later, since the *Sutras* form a more consistent treatise on meditation without it. Whatever their origin, the *Yoga Sutras* are a masterpiece of conciseness and precision. They were handed down orally from teachers to students for generations, before being written down in Sanskrit and later translated for Western readers.

▷ The philosophy of yoga pervades Indian sacred texts, beginning with the Vedas, which are among the world's most ancient scriptures.

ASHTANGA: EIGHT LIMBS
Patanjali defined eight intertwined aspects of yoga, of which the first five are "outer" or active practices. They prepare for the three "inner" limbs which together constitute the meditative state of *samyama*.
Yama: social restraints reflecting an attitude of respect, consideration and love for others, as taught by all the great religions
Niyama: inner purificatory practices reinforcing an attitude of respect for ourselves as embodiments of consciousness
Asana: the perfection of seated postures for meditation, becoming impervious to the opposites (such as heat and cold) that disturb meditation practice
Pranayama: breathing techniques to balance and increase vital energies, used to launch us into meditation
Pratyahara: turning the senses away from the outside world (relaxation) to the world within (witnessing and visualization)
Dharana: focusing techniques to make the mind "one-pointed" and shut out mental chatter
Dhyana: the state of meditation arrived at by maintaining relaxed one-pointedness, using the mind to go beyond the mind
Samadhi: the state of expansion of consciousness that lies beyond the thinking mind

△ Some schools of yoga seek the meditative state primarily through the challenges of the yogasanas (postures).

the teachings of Patanjali's Yoga Sutras

Patanjali follows an ancient Indian philosophy called *samkhya* (dualism). This sees *prakriti* (nature) and *purusha* (consciousness) as forever separate and distinct, and our perceived existence as embodied human beings as a result of the relationship – or "entanglement" – of consciousness with nature.

According to this belief system, the human mind is a part of the colourful, active and ever-changing mirage that is nature. Patanjali describes the human mind in detail, together with the obstacles and suffering we have to contend with. He outlines the illusions that trip us up when we keep entangling consciousness, which is unchanging, within our natural and incessant mental activity: our hopes and fears for the future, and our memories of the past.

Patanjali sets out a wide range of meditation practices, shared by a number of traditions, to train the mind to relax in one-pointed stillness so as to reflect consciousness (the eternal self or spirit) "as a clear crystal". "Yoga is the settling of the mind into silence… [so that] pure unbounded consciousness remains, forever established in its own absolute nature. This is enlightenment" – and the goal of meditation.

There is a detailed section on the eight limbs before the *Sutras* describe at length the extraordinary powers of a mind trained in samyama, or meditation perfectly concentrated on a single object so that the meditator becomes one with the object and perception is transformed.

Finally, Patanjali describes the wonderful state of unclouded truth that is the pinnacle of human perception: "Now the process by which evolution unfolds through time is understood." (Quoted passages from A. Shearer's translation.)

PATANJALI'S MEDITATIONS

Meditative practices recommended by Patanjali include the following, quoted from Alistair Shearer's translation of Patanjali's *Yoga Sutras* (Ch1,v23–39):

- "surrender to the almighty Lord who is the Teacher of even the most ancient tradition of teachers and who is expressed through the sound of the sacred syllable OM"
- "bringing the mind repeatedly to a single focus"
- "cultivating the qualities of the heart: friendliness towards the joyful, compassion towards the suffering, happiness towards the pure, and impartiality towards the impure"
- "[practising] various breathing exercises"
- "experience of the inner radiance which is free from sorrow"
- "attuning to another mind (such as a saint or guru) which is itself unperturbed by desire"
- "the witnessing of dreams" (learning how dreams can access our subconscious levels)
- "any [type of] meditation held in high esteem" (Patanjali recognizes that his way is not the only one)

⊲ The quality of stillness is central to Patanjali's belief system.

Peeling away the layers

◁ The concept of the five koshas gives us a mental map to help us on the spiritual journey inward during meditation.

THE LINE OF COMMAND THROUGH THE KOSHAS

Through meditation we can influence the levels above, as well as the levels below, the one that is the focus of our meditation.

- At soul level (called *ananda maya kosha*, or sheath full of bliss) we form our life's purpose and express this through our attitudes
- which influence our conscious choices (in *vijnana maya kosha*, or sheath full of intellectual understanding)
- which influence our unconscious mental programming (in *mano maya kosha*, or sheath full of mental activity)
- which directs our flow of vital energies (in *prana maya kosha*, or sheath full of life force)
- which move our physical bodies (*anna maya kosha*, or sheath full of food) to perform our actions and behaviour, such as thinking and communicating.

According to the ancient Hindu philosophy of Vedanta, a human being consists of five bodies, each contained within the next, which hide the immortal spirit as if with a series of veils of varying density. These bodies are known as the *koshas*, or "sheaths".

Our progress toward self-realization through meditation can be seen as a journey inward, through each of these five sheaths, from the outermost layer – the physical body – to the deepest "soul body" of unchanging consciousness, where we are in loving touch with all souls.

the five koshas

The further from the physical body they are, the finer the veils become. The most dense of the koshas is perceived by the senses as the structure of the physical body, which can be weighed and measured by scientific instruments.

The next is the energy body, perceptible to clairvoyants, which can be detected by Kirlian photography (a technique that uses a high-voltage, low-current

◁ The koshas can be visualized as the layers of an onion, forming a series of sheaths around the centre.

electric charge to represent the body's energy in visual form). This is the level at which we are aware of the presence of someone entering our "space" before we see them. It contains a web of energy channels meeting at the *chakra* points, or energy centres, that correspond to the concentrations of nerves, or plexuses, of the brain and spinal cord. All physiological processes interact through these channels.

Next comes the "lower" or instinctive mental body. This contains the "mental computer" that is programmed to react

▷ Learning to understand your own nature and shedding negative feelings of fear through the practice of meditation puts you at ease with yourself and makes for trusting, open relationships with others.

according to the input keyed in by our temperament and previous conditioning. The nervous system operates this computer, mostly at instinctive and tribal levels below conscious awareness.

The next level is the veil of the intellect, involved in thinking, discrimination and choice. It can choose to override mental programming, and to respond consciously rather than reacting instinctively.

The finest veil of all, often called the soul body, is linked with the spiritual dimension and survives death. If we can reach this level in meditation, we can change our whole attitude to life and the way we live. This is conscious evolution, opening up the dormant areas of the brain.

instinct, interaction and reasoning

It often seems that different forces co-exist within us, pulling us in opposing directions. This is because we have three distinct brains governing how we behave, feel and think. Our ancient reptilian brain is tiny but very powerful. Situated at the top of the spinal cord, it controls the primitive instincts and urges that ensure physical survival in animal bodies. It drives the basic needs that ensure

our physical and species survival – food, safety, shelter, sleep and procreation. The mammalian brain, above the reptilian brain at the back of the skull, evolved later and processes herd, tribal and social instincts. The rest of the skull contains the most recent development, the neo-cortex. This uniquely human brain enables us to think, reason and evolve spiritually.

The neo-cortex is so new that we use less than ten per cent of it, and it cannot easily override our older brains. However altruistic our intentions, we feel frightened and angry, and may indulge in self-centred behaviour, whenever we consider our basic needs are not being met. We actually need very little to survive, but modern society depends on inflaming our instinctive fear and addictive greed, so that we keep buying the products that keep the wheel turning – unsustainably in the long term.

trusting more, needing less

The practices of meditation help us to balance our evolved and primitive natures. The tradition of Vedanta claims that all creation arises from the desire of the one absolute reality to experience itself as life (nature) and light (consciousness or spirit) in relationship (love) with each other. This relationship is continuously enacted within us, and is seen as the purpose of human existence. The attributes of life, light and love (*sat-chit-ananda*) are immortal, and therefore so are we, as part of the one indivisible whole. Trusting in the divine process of life-light-love creates joy rather than fear and makes the accumulation of things seem less important than expressing our true nature. It is like being protected from negativity by a shield that beams out goodwill to all, while hiding a glory we cannot yet understand.

△ Fear of isolation and exclusion from the crowd can be a result of feeling unhappy with yourself at a fundamental level.

△ Reaching a state of inner content means that you can be happy and relaxed whether you are alone or part of a group.

Freeing vital energies

"It is just as unbalanced to be held fast by material concerns as to be too heavenly to be any earthly use."
Traditional wisdom

In the Eastern traditions (and also in many modern therapeutic systems) it is assumed that our vital energies – or "life force" – flow through the energy channels (*nadis*) of the second kosha (prana maya kosha), or subtle body. Techniques that operate at this level are aimed at healing, balancing and increasing our energies. Yoga postures can get energies flowing when they are sluggish or blocked, while breathing techniques clear and balance the energy channels.

the chakras and granthis

One of the major energy channels follows the spinal cord and links the seven main chakras. The chakras can be thought of as spinning vortices of energy. Breathing with awareness (pranayama) is practised to influence the energies in the chakras and to weaken the three *granthis* (knots of attachment) that bind us to our negative attitudes and prevent us from experiencing the fullness of life-light-love. Although the granthis are seen as obstacles on the path of spiritual awareness, they also act as safety valves, protecting us from surges of vital energy and misplaced enthusiasm for changes we are not ready for. We need to practise well-tried and tested methods (such as meditation) to open them slowly and naturally, rather than forcing them with drugs or stimulants.

△ Yoga postures use movement and stretches to tone the physical body and stimulate the chakras and the connecting energy channels.

▷ The chakras are often described as lotus flowers; meditation makes them bloom and perfume our lives with their positive attributes.

The energies of all the koshas are expressed in each chakra. We can behave spiritually in practical ways from the base chakra, or serve the divine efficiently from the crown chakra. However we behave, feel or think we cannot help bringing life and

◁ The granthis are visualized as three knots that bind us to negative attitudes and material concerns, keeping our minds and spirits closed. The granthis constrict the free flow of energy that leads to true understanding and acceptance.

light together in the relationship of love – even if we can perceive only conflict and fear. Awareness is the key to all meditation practice, so we must first "switch on the light" in the brow (mind) chakra before doing anything else, through breathing techniques that quickly "light us up".

Life chakras and the life granthi

The life chakras correspond to the positions of the nerve plexuses attached to the spine behind the abdomen. Their energies are concerned with our survival in the physical human body (the base chakra, connected to the legs and feet), our role in human society (the sacral chakra) and our sense of self-esteem as a human personality (the navel chakra). The life granthi that binds us is our attachment to material wellbeing, physical comforts and luxuries, and the amassing of things. Patanjali teaches self-discipline for regulating the energy through the life chakras and life granthi.

Love chakras and the love granthi

The love chakras are situated in the chest (the heart chakra, connected to arms and hands) and neck (the throat chakra, connected to voice, mouth and hearing). In this area self-concern gives way to sharing with others. The heart chakra energies are concerned with relationship – especially unconditional love – and the throat chakra with expressing the truth and hearing what others are telling us. The love granthi that binds us is our attachment to emotional excitement and the desire to be the hero of every drama, so that we are not receptive to the needs of others. Patanjali teaches self-surrender for increasing the energy through the love chakras and love granthi.

Light chakras and the light granthi

The light chakras are situated in the skull. They are the brow chakra (connected to the mind) and the crown chakra (connected to the spirit). "Taking the mind into the heart" is an essential element of meditation, bringing the realization that relating, not thinking, is the purpose of life. The light of divinity is received through the crown chakra and is present in us as "the eternal flame burning in the cave of the heart". The light granthi that binds us is our attachment to our own opinions, prejudices and fantasies. It is hard to relinquish treasured opinions and pride in our own intellect, yet it is not our minds but the light and love in our hearts that make us divine. We cannot claim ownership of universal life-light-love. Patanjali teaches self-awareness to dissolve pride and those mental habits that obscure divine light.

THE CHAKRAS

The base chakra (*muladhara*) is concerned with survival.

The sacral chakra (*svadisthana*) is related to our role in human society.

The navel chakra (*manipura*) is related to energy and self-esteem.

◁ The seven main chakras are represented in a line running up the spinal column. Each is traditionally associated with a colour.

The heart chakra (*anahata*) is concerned with relationships.

The throat chakra (*vishuddhi*) is related to communication.

The brow chakra (*ajna*), also known as the third eye, is related to intuition.

The crown chakra (*sahasrara*) is related to spiritual understanding.

Achieving balance and harmony

◁ The play of the gunas can be compared to the skills needed by a tightrope walker, who combines movement with stillness to create harmony, focus, balance and beauty.

lacking in hope. A tamasic attitude among those in power – such as bureaucrats or those running businesses – will perpetuate laziness, procrastination, ignorance and lack of concern.

However, even though tamas is a "constipating" quality that can block progress in both individuals and institutions, it is also characterized by resilience and staying power. Inertia also has its positive side – we all need to take time out for rest, sleep and recuperation when our systems are depleted. Tamasic feelings of lethargy and dullness can be a sign of exhaustion or illness, and may be the body's warning to stop or suffer the consequences.

THE BALANCE OF OPPOSITES

There is a correspondence between the interaction of the three gunas, or qualities of nature, and the three attributes of the absolute or non-nature (light-life-love), in that when the two opposites merge in a balanced state a third quality arises that contains and transcends both opposites. The principle seems to underlie the way things work at the deepest levels. Some examples are:

- Sat/existence (life) + chit/consciousness (light) = ananda/bliss (love)
- Tamas (inertia) + rajas (motion) = sattva (equilibrium)
- Patanjali's self-discipline + self-awareness = self-surrender
- Male + female = a new being
- Day + night = time

All aspects of nature possess inner properties called *gunas*, which are described at length in many of the ancient texts of India. There are three gunas, all of which are present in varying proportions in everything, from the human mind to the food we eat, but the dominance of one of them characterizes everything in the physical world. According to the dualistic philosophy of samkhya, this imbalance between the gunas is a result of the disturbance caused by Creation.

tamas

The first guna is *tamas*, the state of darkness, silence and ignorance, where nothing happens. In scientific terms, tamas is inertia. This quality receives much abuse in the texts because it blocks any attempt to change and therefore obstructs evolution.

The tamasic state of mind is lethargic, selfish and dull. When we are dominated by tamas we are lacking in energy, fearful and dependent on other people, regretful and

> "The difference between the best and worst of us is nothing compared to that between what we are and what we will become."
> *Traditional wisdom*

rajas

Opposed to the tamasic state is *rajas*, the quality of desire, arousal and passion – or motion. Rajas is an epidemic in Western society. We are urged to want more, to buy everything on credit and to work harder and longer to pay for the luxuries we think are necessities. Our nervous systems are whipped into a constant state of "red alert", so that we rush around ever faster to fight or flee imaginary threats. A rajasic attitude perpetuates fear, greed, delusion, desire and many other exhausting stimuli.

Although rajas causes addiction, obsession, dissipation of energy and burnout, it also has its positive aspects. Without zeal, ardour and drive nothing in life can be achieved. The spiritual path requires intense and ongoing commitment.

△ Meditation practice helps us to achieve a balance in our lives between activity and rest, interaction and solitude, fostering inner peace and loving relationships.

sattva

When the two opposite qualities of tamas and rajas blend together, *sattva* is created, the state of balance and harmony – or equilibrium. This quality combines the best aspects of the other two, making us relaxed yet energetic, trusting and accepting yet innovative and creative, committed to goals yet unattached to outcomes. Needless to say, sattva is the quality we aim for as the preparation for meditation – for when we are lethargic it is hard to maintain focus and when we are obsessive it is hard to maintain non-attachment.

PATANJALI'S THREE PRELIMINARY PRACTICES

Patanjali defines three qualities we need to develop before we can enter the meditative state. Each makes us more mindful of the dominance of tamas or rajas within us, and helps us to bring them into balance to achieve the inner harmony of sattva.

- **Self-discipline (*tapas*)** which removes the inertia and procrastination that is typical of tamas, which can block us when we plan to do our practices. Nothing is achieved without disciplined commitment.
- **Self-awareness (*swadhyaya*)**, enables us to discover patterns of rajas and tamas as we witness our thoughts, feelings, reactions and behaviour throughout the day without involvement or excuses. Patanjali also prescribes the study of uplifting texts, to learn from enlightened saints and sages.
- **Self-surrender (*ishwara pranidhana*)** to a higher power than the drives and resistances of our own personalities. We may picture this power as a divine person or as an impersonal source, fullness or void.

Through self-discipline and self-awareness we let go of the attachments represented by the three granthis and free ourselves to reach our potential.

△ The rajasic character (left), prevalent in Western society, is turbulent and excitable and impatient, whereas dullness and indifference characterize the tamasic state (right).

△ When the opposing qualities of rajas and tamas are in balance with each other, the result is the sattvic state: happy, alert, clear-thinking and compassionate.

Preparing Body and Mind

The most external levels of our being are our physical body and our energy flow. Through a sequence of gentle movements and techniques that foster awareness of the breath, we can bring both these levels into a state of harmony, so that we can sit comfortably and peacefully for meditation practice. Exercises that slow and deepen the breathing bring a "feel-good" factor to the body, while also relaxing and resting the mind, and traditional postures for meditation allow energy to flow freely as we start to turn our focus inward.

Basic body and breath awareness

The traditional position for meditation practice is to sit with the knees out to each side. This creates a pyramid with a firm triangular base so that it is difficult to topple over and easy to keep the spine erect, even when you are totally engrossed in inner experiences. However, in Western society we seldom sit in this position.

Although the hips, like the shoulders, are ball-and-socket joints, designed to turn freely in all directions, we normally move through a very narrow range of standing and sitting positions. Imagine how restricted you would feel if you could move your elbows only up or down in front of you but not to the sides – yet this is what we do with our knees as we sit at a desk and in a car or armchair, while walking or running, and even when we are lying down. In ancient India it would have been as natural and comfortable to sit cross-legged on the floor as sitting in an armchair is for us, and with gentle practice and suitable props you can enjoy the benefits of this pose and also regain a more natural range of movement in your hip joints.

breath with posture and movement

In exercise, moving with the breath brings a new mental awareness and a feeling of both relaxation and energy flow, so it is important to develop the habit of leading every movement with a conscious slow breath either in or out, as directed.

Do the exercises suggested for just a few moments, as frequently as possible during the day. Relax and enjoy them, and never force your body into any position. You will be amazed how quickly you begin to shed the tightness that has been restricting your body for years. A relaxed body and mind creates a wonderful sense of wellbeing and makes meditation practice very rewarding.

Start by standing in the classical Tadasana pose – feet parallel and a little apart, ankles lifted, knees straight and springy (not locked), tailbone (coccyx) tucked under, waist pulled in and back, breastbone (sternum) lifted, chin parallel to the floor. The gaze is soft and straight ahead. Imagine a straight line down each side of your body. It should pass through your ankles, knees, hips, waist, shoulders and ears. Having located all these points, breathe in to stretch up, and out to bring them into line. You should feel as though you are hanging from the ceiling by a strong cord, with your limbs loose like a puppet. The same exercise – stretching up on the breath in and aligning on the breath out – can be practised while seated on a chair or on the floor.

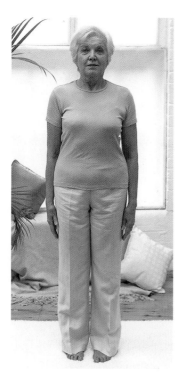

△ In Tadasana, the mountain pose, the body extends upward from a firm base, with the sides, front and back of the body aligned, creating a sense of equilibrium and repose.

USING YOGA POSES
The classical yoga poses (asanas), are designed to promote strength, flexibility, balance, breath awareness, relaxation and focus. This makes them ideal exercises for all the koshas, and an excellent preparation for meditation. However, provided it is performed with the same awareness, any gentle stretching can also exercise all the koshas.

△ Vrksasana, the "tree" pose, is one of the classic yoga postures used in preparation for meditation practice.

swing a leg

This exercise, repeated frequently at odd moments during the day, releases muscular tension, improves balance and develops body awareness. At the end of the sequence, quietly observe everything you can feel in your body.

△ **1** Standing in Tadasana, become comfortable with your breath, awareness and posture, so that you can maintain them throughout the exercise. If your balance is shaky, stand where you can hold on to a table, the back of a chair, or a wall if you need to.

△ **2** Raise one leg, bending the knee, until the thigh is parallel to the floor. Balance on the other leg, using your breath to stretch up and align your body, and to hold the position. When you are balanced, shake your raised ankle gently and rhythmically.

△ **3** After a moment, change the movement so that you are swinging the lower part of the raised leg, from the knee, with the ankle relaxed. Continue to focus on the breath, and maintain the Tadasana pose.

△ **4** Now swing the whole of the raised leg from the hip, forward and back, keeping it relaxed and maintain the Tadasana pose. Take a deep breath in, then breathe out, as you lower your leg and stand on it. Breathe in to raise the other thigh parallel to the floor and repeat the sequence.

deep standing squat

This exercise brings awareness and strength to the legs and back. Loosen the muscles around the hip, knee and ankle joints by practising a few squats frequently.

"The physical postures should be steady and comfortable. They are mastered when all effort is relaxed and the mind is absorbed in the Infinite."
From A. Shearer's translation of Patanjali's Sutras, Ch2

△ **1** Stand at arms' length in front of a stable object, such as a chair or table, and grasp it firmly for support as you squat. Your feet should be comfortably apart and turned out at 45 degrees, so that your ankles, knees and hips are in alignment when you sink down into the squat. Keep your spine erect and your gaze forward.

△ **2** Breathe in and stretch up through your spine and neck, then breathe out while gently squatting down as low as is comfortable for you. Keep your heels on the floor if you can, or raise them until your lower back becomes more flexible. Breathe in to rise and out again to repeat the squat.

Opening up the chakras

Gentle stretches and movements, working with the breath, help to release muscular tension in the physical body and also to free obstructions at the energy level. Breathing up through the body from the floor, and down from above the head, increases the energy in the spine, which flows through the chakras.

increasing vitality

The knees, hips and pelvis are all part of the "life" area of the body, where the centres that process vitality are located. The legs and the base of the spine are under the influence of the base chakra, and the hips and pelvis are under the influence of the sacral chakra. Seated stretches and bends energize these two chakras. If you add a twist to your movement you will be activating the navel chakra as well.

opening the chest

Exercises that open up the chest will foster improved breathing and better posture, and these can be done in a standing, kneeling or sitting position.

To start, the breath in is focused upon stretching up. If you are standing or kneeling, this stretch begins through the legs, then continues through the lower, middle and upper spine, and the neck. The upward stretch opens your chest to create space for deeper breathing and improves your posture by lengthening your spine to allow increased energy flow through the chakras, including the heart chakra in the chest and the throat chakra above. The breath out – done with the same relaxed attention – can be focused into movements involving the limbs, while still maintaining the strength and openness of the spine and neck.

By linking your breath with movement in these exercises, you are working from within, rather than making the correct "shapes" as seen from outside. In this way you can release physical tension and mental and emotional stress with every combined breath and movement. It is best to start with simple movements in order to focus on this co-ordination of mind and body with the rhythm of the breath.

Every nerve impulse that passes between the brain and the body has to travel through the neck, so it is very helpful to release any tension that has built up in this area. Continue the upward stretch of the spine through the neck and into the skull, and maintain the stretch during the movements to open the chest. At the same time, be aware of any tension in the throat and face and keep them relaxed.

wide-angled seated movements

The more you sit on the floor with your legs comfortably wide apart and practise these movements, the more quickly your hips, lower back and spine will release the muscular tension that is so restrictive and can also cause pain and malfunction.

△ **1** Twist for navel chakra: sit on a cushion with your back straight and legs apart, toes pointing to the ceiling and the backs of your knees relaxed on the floor (though tight hamstring muscles may keep the legs bent to begin with). Breathe in and stretch the spine up. With your right hand on your left thigh, breathe out, twisting your trunk to the left and your left shoulder round behind you. Breathe in to return to the centre and stretch up. Breathe out to change sides. Repeat several times.

△ **2** Side bend for sacral chakra: breathe in and stretch up. Place one hand on each thigh. As you breathe out, slide your right hand down your right leg and look up to the left, bringing your left shoulder back to open the left side of the chest area. Breathe in to straighten up and repeat on the other side. Repeat several times.

△ **3** Forward bend for base and sacral chakras: place your fingertips on the floor in front of you and gently "walk" them forward, keeping your spine stretched. Avoid rounding your back and jutting your chin forward to reach further than is comfortable, as this causes tense muscles, whereas relaxation loosens them. Breathe in to stretch right through your spine. As you breathe out, sink forward a little more. As you relax deeply, you may want to rest your head in your hands with your elbows on the floor and smile. Come up again gently and slowly.

opening the book

This can be done standing, seated or kneeling. It is important to keep the chest open and the breastbone (sternum) lifted. The upper spine and neck are stretched up, strong and unmoving, and the elbows are at shoulder level as you move the arms.

▷ **1** Stand "tall", stretching through the spine, with palms joined in front of your body and elbows at shoulder height. Breathe out for this "closing" position, stretching your ribcage at the back.

△ **2** Breathe in to "open the book", bringing your elbows (still at shoulder height) to the sides, palms facing forward. The spine and neck should not move at all as you press the elbows right back. Repeat the movement several times.

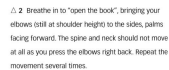

elbow rotations

As with all arm movements, the spine and neck are not involved and need to be held firmly in position throughout.

▷ **1** Place your fingertips on your shoulders and, keeping your breastbone lifted, bring your elbows in front of your body, as high as possible. Breathe out for this "closing" position, stretching your ribcage at the back.

△ **2** Breathing in, rotate your elbows up, round and back, squeezing your shoulderblades together and stretching your ribs at the sides. Your spine and neck should remain stretched up and unmoving. Repeat several times, then circle your elbows the other way.

chest expansion

It is important to keep the spine and neck stretched up and unmoving as the arms are raised and lowered. This is an isometric exercise (developing muscle strength without moving) for the spine and neck and an isotonic exercise (stretching and moving) for the arms and the pectoral muscles in the chest.

> "Open the window in the centre of your chest and let spirit move in and out."
>
> *Rumi, 13th century*

△ **1** Clasp your hands behind your back, keeping the palms firmly pressed together all the time. As you breathe in, push your clasped hands down toward the floor, squeezing your shoulderblades together.

△ **2** As you breathe out, raise your straight arms up behind you, keeping the palms firmly pressed together. Repeat several times. Even if only a little movement is possible at first, this is a powerful exercise, and you will find that your range of movement will increase with practice.

Learning to let go

The combination of relaxed stretching and deep, slow breathing is a quick and effective way to settle the "bodymind" in preparation for meditation. You can practise the following stretches and breathing techniques at any time of the day – preferably several times during each day. The resulting reduction in your stress levels will be gradual but cumulative. The practice leads to a calmer mind, clearer thinking, a more comfortable, relaxed body and a more open-hearted acceptance of the way things are – including the inadequacies of other people and of yourself.

active preparation

Of the eight limbs in Patanjali's system of raja yoga, the yoga of meditation, five are "outer" (*bahir*) or active limbs. All five physical aspects are to be practised together, and all are necessary to remove tensions from the body, emotions and mind, in order to experience the meditative state.

If we are angry with someone, or discontented with ourselves, or unable to sit still, or struggling with unhealthy breathing patterns and high stress levels, or if our minds are distracted by outer sensory stimuli and constant inner chatter, it is

impossible to give our full attention to meditation practice. Patanjali's first two limbs reinforce an attitude of respect and care for others through social restraint (yama) and for ourselves through purification (niyama). These are followed by a firm, comfortable seated position (asana) for meditation practice, breathing exercises (pranayama) to balance and increase energy, and finally relaxation and "switching off" (pratyahara). Only then are we ready to practise the three "inner" (*antar*) limbs that make up samyama (these are concentration, meditation and absorption/ecstasy).

skiing

This exercise stretches and flexes all the muscles that hold the spine, releasing tension and tightness that may be restricting blood flow, nerve communications and energy flow. It also opens the front of the chest and makes the breastbone more flexible, for better breathing.

△ **1** Stand with your feet comfortably apart and parallel. Bend your knees and squat right down, stretching your arms out in front of you for balance. Lift your arms, opening your chest, as you breathe in. Imagine you are holding two ski poles and plant them firmly in the snow ahead of you.

△ **2** Breathing out, sweep your arms down and back, reaching as high behind you as you can to wave your imaginary ski poles in the air after they have propelled you forward. Repeat this movement several times. The visualization of the movement should make you feel flushed with exertion and enjoyment.

△ **3** When you feel you have done enough skiing, squat down with your arms and trunk between your knees and rest. Breathe naturally and feel the weight of your body stretching your lower back and legs.

easing the spine and neck

When you exercise lying down, gravity supports and cradles you, so these exercises are very soothing – especially if you feel stiff or have painful twinges in your lower back, hips or neck. You may feel more comfortable lying on your back if you place a small cushion under your head (not your neck) to lengthen your neck and bring your chin down toward your chest. Keep your neck area free, so that it can stretch.

△ **1** Bend your knees on to your chest and clasp your hands around your shins (or the backs of your thighs). Breathing out, curl up your spine to bring your nose or forehead (not your chin, as this constricts your neck) to touch your knees. Breathe in to replace your head on the cushion, with your chin tucked in. Breathe out to begin the sequence again and repeat several times.

△ **2** To ease your lower back and hips, lie with your bent knees comfortably apart and one hand on each knee, with your elbows resting on the floor if possible. This is an open and relaxed pose that can ease pain from trapped nerves (such as sciatica). Breathing deeply and naturally, use your hands to circle your knees in toward each other then out to the sides in slow circles, really relaxing all your back and leg muscles.

△ **3** Keeping your spine relaxed and knees wide and supported by your hands, with elbows resting on the floor, take your full attention to your neck. Breathing out slowly, turn your head to one side and turn your eyes to look at the floor.

△ **4** Breathe in to raise your head and eyes to the centre and out to turn them to the other side. Repeat several times, focusing on awareness and relaxation of all your neck muscles. Keep your spine, legs, arms and jaw completely relaxed throughout.

△ **5** Bring your arms overhead, clasping your hands loosely if you can, or simply bringing your bent arms as high as possible – your elbows should be relaxed on the floor. This position stretches the front of your body. Place your feet together on the floor close to your buttocks, and relax your upper body, neck and jaw. You will move only from the waist down. Breathe in and, as you breathe out, drop your knees (keeping them pressed together) to the floor on your right side. Breathe in to raise your knees and out to lower them to the left.

△ **6** For extra strengthening of the upper inner thighs – essential for good posture – press a sheet of paper between your knees and hold it there as you move your knees from side to side.

Breathing techniques

Focusing on the breath is a universal technique for enlightenment and healing, and many traditions use breathing practices either as a way to prepare for meditation or as meditation techniques in themselves. Conscious control of the breath, or pranayama, is the fourth limb of Patanjali's system. The technique of holding the breath – either in or out – is beyond the scope of this book, as accomplishing it safely requires one-to-one teaching, but becoming aware of the breathing process and directing the flow of the breath is within the capacity of everyone.

Slowing down the breathing and lengthening the breath out (which is what happens when we sing or chant) switches the nervous system into its peaceful happy mode, allowing stress to be dissolved and rest, digestion, absorption and healing to take place at every level of the five koshas.

Patanjali's path to enlightenment

This use of the breath fits in perfectly with Patanjali's philosophy. He describes three vital steps (which have been called "preliminary purificatory practices") that encapsulate his path to enlightenment. The steps are as follows (quote marks refer to the translation of Patanjali's *Sutras* by Alistair Shearer, Ch2, v1/2):

"Purification" [through self-discipline]
"Refinement" [through self-awareness]
"Surrender" [through self-surrender and
* continual letting-go]*
"These are the practical steps on the path of yoga."
They nourish the state of samadhi
* [absorption/ecstasy/expansion]*
"And weaken the causes of suffering."

The whole process of self-development starts with taking conscious control over our own nervous system, so that we experience more "expansion" and joy and less stress and unhappiness. Our circumstances influence the outcome of events far less than our own basic attitudes, and these can be changed from negative to positive by the simple act of changing our breathing pattern.

The breath forms part of the energy system and the physiological processes in the energy kosha, while nervous energy runs the mental computer in the kosha of unconscious programming. All the koshas meet and blend in the chakra system in the energy kosha and all can therefore be consciously influenced through the practices of breathing and meditation.

Although some translations of the *Yoga Sutras* describe Patanjali's three "purificatory steps" as "preliminary", there is really no end to our need of them. We always have to maintain our discipline and keep our attention focused - and we never stop needing to let go of something or other.

> "Those who see a glass as half empty feel deprived, whereas those who see it as half full feel blessed."
> *Traditional wisdom*

viloma: focusing on the breathing muscles

This useful focusing technique can be practised anywhere, sitting with the spine erect and the hands and eyes still.

▷ **1** Place your hands on your knees, palms either up or down, with thumb and index fingers touching to close the energy circuits. As you breathe in deeply, feel your ribs expand and your diaphragm contract downward against your stomach. Notice how these movements cause air to flow into your lungs.

2 As you breathe out, count "One and two and...", then stop your breath in mid-flow for the same count. Repeat until you have slowly and comfortably expelled enough air, then repeat this cycle four times more and rest. Then reverse the cycle, breathing in and counting "One and two and..." Pause and repeat until the lungs feel full, then breathe out slowly. Repeat four times more. Use the fractional breath in to start your day or whenever you need energy, and the fractional breath out to relax before meditation.

WATCHPOINTS FOR BREATHING PRACTICE

Regular practice will calm the mind and raise your energy levels. As the lungs strengthen, their capacity will be increased. Practise little and often – a few rounds of the breathing exercises now and then throughout the day will prepare you for longer sessions during meditation practice.

- Avoid any breathing practices after meals – when your stomach is full it presses against your diaphragm, constricting your lungs.
- Keep your spine stretched and as straight as possible (allowing for its natural curves) whether you are standing, sitting, kneeling or lying down to practise breathing. This allows maximum lung expansion and helps the free flow of both air and energy.
- Keep your breastbone lifted to open your chest and give your diaphragm room to move freely. Keep it lifted even when breathing out, letting your diaphragm and rib muscles do all the work.
- Always breathe in through your nose, as it is the filter that protects your lungs from cold, dust and infections from outside. Breathe out through your nose unless you are making sounds.
- Develop your focus on, and conscious awareness of, your breathing patterns, so that you constantly monitor their effects upon you. Develop the habit of watching yourself breathing.
- Slow your breathing down – especially your breath out – whenever you feel agitated or anxious, in order to gain conscious control over your autonomic nervous system.
- Stop your breathing practice and rest for a few natural breaths the instant you feel breathless. Start again when your nervous system has settled down and relaxed. It is not used to being watched and controlled, as breathing is usually an unconscious process.

alternate nostril breathing

This universally popular exercise quickly balances the nervous system, so that you feel calm and centred after just a few rounds – ready either for meditation practice or to get on with your day refreshed.

△ **1** Sit erect with your left hand on your knee or in your lap. Raise your right hand to place it against your face. Your thumb will close your right nostril, your index and middle fingers will rest aginst your forehead at the brow chakra and your ring finger will close your left nostril.

△ **2** Your eyes may be closed, or open and gazing softly ahead. Keep your eyeballs still, as quiet eyes induce a quiet mind. Close your right nostril with your thumb. Breathe in through the left nostril.

△ **3** Release the right nostril and close the left with your ring finger. Breathe out slowly, and then in again, through your right nostril. Then open the left nostril, close the right and breathe out. This is one round. Do five rounds, breathe naturally to rest, then repeat a few times.

double breathing

This exercise fosters your self-awareness and observation. It also tones the muscles that give you "core strength" and support your spine, giving you increased energy and stamina for self-discipline, and improving posture and energy flow. Start each round by breathing in from your feet up (if you are standing), or from the base of your spine if you are sitting.

△ **1** Bring your palms together at chest level with elbows wide, lifting your breastbone and drawing your spine erect. Breathe slowly and deeply a few times to settle yourself.

△ **2** Point your fingers downward and focus on the base of your body. As you breathe in, tighten the muscles of your upper inner thighs and pelvic floor, and at the same time draw your lower abdominal muscles back toward your spine. This movement lifts your life energy upward.

△ **3** As you breathe out, turn your hands so your fingers point toward your collarbones, at the base of your throat, lifting your elbows to shoulder level. At the same time draw your energy up from the base, through the waist as you tighten your abdominal "corset muscles", and up to your head as you lift your chin. In this position breathe in, opening your ribs at the back of your chest by pressing your palms firmly together, as you bring spiritual energy down into your heart centre. Breathe out as you lower your fingertips and take your energy to the floor. Repeat the cycle twice more, then rest.

◁ Breathing practices can be done in a kneeling position if you find this comfortable. The pose creates a strong, stable base and helps to keep the spine erect to maximize the flow of energy. When you are kneeling or sitting, start the upward breath in from the base of your spine.

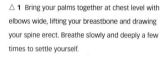

"We can keep only what we are prepared to surrender."
Traditional wisdom

grounding ritual

This is an essential step at the end of your meditation, so that you clear your mind of all you have experienced and go back to daily life refreshed and in "active mode", rather than "heady" and "spaced out". It is an exercise in self-surrender, as you give to the earth all the relaxation and joy you feel as a result of your meditation practice. This is one reason why we meditate – to share positive energy with those with whom we interact.

△ **1** At the end of your visualization or other meditation practice, bring your palms together and breathe in, mentally giving heartfelt thanks for the experience, whatever it was like for you.

△ **2** As you breathe out, fold forward to ground yourself by placing your hands on the floor – and your head also if you can reach – giving to the earth all the experience and benefit you have received.

bee buzzing breath

This technique uses sound to begin extending the length of the breath out. It induces instant relaxation and reduction of stress, and is an exercise in "letting go".

△ **1** Sit erect, placing your thumbs in position ready to close your ear flaps, and your fingers ready to close your eyelids and lips.

2 Breathe in deeply. As you breathe out, "close down" and make a humming sound like a bee. Feel this sound vibrating through your body, loosening tightness and tension. Before you run out of breath, open your eyes and ears to breathe in and repeat.

△ **Explore the physical effects of your breath on your abdominal organs by placing your hands on the sides of your ribs, then on the front and finally on your lower abdomen.**

Posture principles

Meditation practices are traditionally performed sitting with the spine erect and vertical, so that energy flows between the "heaven" (light) and "earth" (life) poles of our being. Energy needs to flow smoothly up and down through the physical spine and the energy channels of the subtle body, so that the brain and breathing function optimally and the chakras are balanced and full of vitality. An erect spine is quite easy to maintain if the right props are used to begin with and the right exercises are performed regularly to strengthen the muscles that hold the spine erect and open the hip joints.

meditation and relaxation

Relaxation is quite different from meditation. It is part of the fifth limb of Patanjali's system – pratyahara, or withdrawal of the senses from outer stimuli. Relaxation practices are done lying down in as comfortable a position as possible. Western psychotherapists usually favour a reclining position because their techniques require the client to be relaxed as they follow a guided visualization or answer questions about their past. Meditation practice takes us deeper than this, with the mind quietly focused on a single object. Relaxation – like physical stretching and awareness of breathing – is very useful as a preparation for meditative practice but should not be confused with it.

sitting on a chair

When starting to practise meditation, most Westerners find it easiest to sit upright on a firm chair. Your thighs should be parallel to the floor – in order to achieve this you may need to raise your feet (without shoes) by resting them on a cushion. Sit erect with your hands, palms down, resting on your thighs, hands and feet parallel and pointing forward. This posture is known as the "Egyptian position". If you lean back at all you will quickly develop a backache, so sit

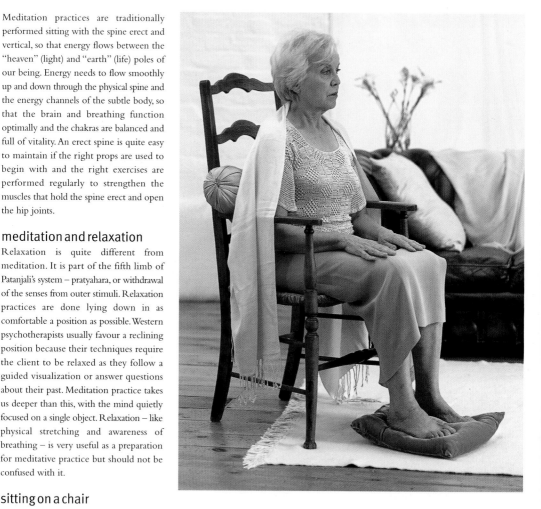

erect with the base of your spine pressed against the chair back or a firm cushion.

Once you are settled in this position you can gradually increase the time you can comfortably remain motionless. Spend up to ten minutes watching your natural breath or practising breathing exercises to centre your energies along the axis of the spine. You will feel energized and relaxed as a result. Later you may wish to sit motionless for half an hour or longer while you practise

△ **If you choose to sit in a chair for meditation practice, make sure it gives firm support and is a suitable height. Your spine should remain erect, with your head and neck aligned.**

your meditation techniques. If the seated position suits you, you may decide always to practise meditation seated on a particular chair, or you may want to try out a variety of positions as your hips become more flexible through regular stretching exercises.

△ Lack of spinal strength and the right support result in poor posture, with the head jutting forward and the spine rounded. The neck automatically shortens and tenses when the back is humped in this way, constricting the flow of energy, and it is impossible to maintain the position comfortably for the whole period of meditation practice.

△ Good posture results from choosing the right position. The head and neck are aligned and erect, and the spine is vertical. To prevent strain and help with alignment, the base of the spine can be supported on a firm cushion or a folded blanket positioned between the feet.

sitting on the floor

This is the traditional Eastern way to meditate, since chairs were not used in homes until very recently. As a result, people had very flexible hips, so sitting cross-legged on a cushion on the floor was easy and natural. Most Westerners first need to loosen up their hip joints – which has the additional benefit that it reduces the risk of developing arthritic hips in old age. Meanwhile, it is better to sit on a chair, or on your heels in the yogic Vajrasana pose, than with a slumped spine in an attempt to sit with crossed legs on the floor. Whatever position you adopt, do use support where it is needed until your muscles and joints have strengthened and loosened enough for you to be comfortable without support. Many excellent meditation stools and chairs are available, some of which are illustrated in this book.

WHERE SUPPORT MAY BE NEEDED

Your spine may need help in order to remain comfortably erect. You can sit supported by a cushion against a wall – if you are on the floor or in bed – or with a cushion against the back of a firm upright chair (not an armchair). Sitting on your heels may be the easiest way to learn to sit erect without support.

Your hips may not yet open freely enough to allow your knees to rest on the floor in a cross-legged pose. Cushions supporting your thighs will help you to stretch up through your lower back and a firm cushion under your tailbone will relieve pressure in the lower back by lowering your knees. Strategically placed cushions can make sitting on the floor the most comfortable option.

△ A cushion under the tailbone eases the lower back by lifting the hips.

Choosing a posture

Regular practice is the best teacher, as your body quickly gets used to the new routine and settles into it more and more easily. When you find a position that is comfortable for you, practise sitting in it until you can remain motionless, relaxed yet alert, for half an hour or more. It is helpful to vary your position when you sit at home, or to change purposefully from one position to another without disturbing your inner focus whenever your muscles begin to ache. This is much better than focusing on the complaints coming from your body when you push it to sit too long without moving.

△ You may find it helpful to attend a meditation class, where you can be shown different ways to sit and try out the various props available before buying any of them for yourself.

easy cross-legged pose

This involves sitting erect with hips loose and knees wide. Each foot is tucked under the opposite thigh so that the weight of the legs rests on the feet rather than the knees. Place cushions under each thigh and/or under the buttocks if you feel pressure in the lower back. The tailbone (coccyx) should hang freely, letting the "sitting bones" take the weight of the trunk. Place your hands on your knees or rest them in your lap with palms facing up.

◁ If the hips are not sufficiently flexible for the knees to rest on the floor when sitting cross-legged, support them with a couple of cushions. Resting the hands palms up enables you to hold a mala, or rosary.

▷ This low chair, which folds for easy carrying, is specially designed for meditation. It supports the back when sitting in the cross-legged pose. The hands are in *gyana mudra*, with the tips of thumb and forefinger joined to complete the energy circuit.

Buddhist position

The yogic kneeling pose called Virasana is sometimes used for meditation. Buddhists often choose to sit on a very firm cushion that lifts the hips, with the knees resting on the floor on each side of the cushion and the shins and feet pointing back. Lifting the hips in this way helps to keep the spine correctly aligned, and this position can be very comfortable as long as your knees are fairly flexible.

◁ Using a "kneeling" chair helps to keep the spine straight and gives a good, well-supported position that is similar to the Buddhist kneeling pose.

▷ While sitting on a firm cushion in Virasana, the knees and feet can also be supported on a larger cushion. The meditator sits between the feet, rather than on the heels. The hands are in the gesture called *bhairavi mudra*, to focus the energy for meditation.

early morning meditation

Many people like to meditate first thing every morning, while the mind is quiet and before the events of the day have a chance to distract it. If you meditate in bed, use a V-shaped pillow or ordinary pillows to support your back, so that you can sit erect in a cross-legged position. Wear a shawl round your shoulders and pull up the bedclothes so that you feel warm while you are doing your meditation practice. Choose a practice that energizes rather than relaxes you, such as chanting or repeating a mantra using a mala. You may prefer to keep your eyes open in a soft gaze.

▷ Your bed can be a haven of peace and warmth if you prefer to meditate on waking in the morning.

▽ A V-shaped pillow helps you to maintain an erect posture while meditating in bed. A mala, used for counting the repetitions of a mantra, is traditionally kept concealed in its special bag when not in use.

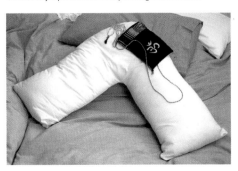

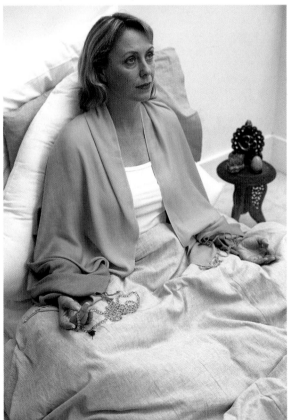

The time, the place

It takes determination to establish a new habit and to make room in your life for a new regular activity. It helps if you train your mind to meditate routinely at a specific time and place. You may still be tempted sometimes to skip your meditation slot and do something else instead, but you will begin to feel uncomfortable when you miss your practice. There will be days when you have to forgo your normal routine, but that will be a conscious decision rather than simply forgetting or procrastinating.

◁ Your "meditation corner" may contain a number of objects on which to focus: any object can act as a trigger to put you in the right frame of mind for your practice.

▷ A crescent-shaped "moon cushion" is often used as support when sitting for meditation.

meditating at a regular time

It is helpful to place your meditation practice in the context of long-established habits – such as before showering in the morning, or after cleaning your teeth, or before lunch or supper. Since you do all these things daily you will meditate daily as well. A good time is when you wake up or before a meal – after meals people are apt to feel sleepy – or in the evening after a brisk walk or listening to soothing music. You might read an uplifting book in bed and then meditate before going to sleep. Choose a time when you are normally alone and undisturbed – the fuller your day, the more rewarding and de-stressing your meditation session can be. Couples often meditate together at a mutually convenient time, or get up early before the household is awake. Whatever time you choose, stick to it to establish your meditation habit.

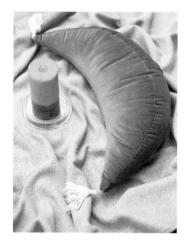

creating a meditation corner

If you always do your meditation in the same place this will also help to establish your meditation habit. Choose a quiet and uncluttered space so that the moment you sit there your mind becomes calm and focused. Make sure you will be warm enough, as body temperature drops when you relax and turn inward.

Your "meditation corner" might consist of a special chair in a peaceful part of your home, or perhaps you might sit on a

MEDITATION IN BED

If you practise meditation in the early morning your bed (with a warm shawl around you and the covers pulled up) can become your "meditation corner". Have a wash, a drink and a good stretch to really wake you up first – and make sure you sit with your spine erect.

If you regularly meditate in bed in the morning, and this is the place where you are in the habit of turning your mind inward, it can also be very soothing to perform simple meditation techniques before you go to sleep at night.

△ When you wake up, have a relaxed, "releasing" stretch before starting your early morning meditation.

△ Last thing at night, relax with your mala and repeat a mantra or simple prayer before you go peacefully to sleep.

△ If you choose to meditate sitting on the floor, a low table is useful for holding objects on which you wish to focus your gaze.

postural stretch

If you have been sitting all day in a car or at your desk, you may want to regain a strong upright posture before you start an evening meditation session. You could try standing with a weighty object on your head to strengthen the spinal column and improve your sense of balance. Previous generations learned "deportment" by walking around the room balancing piles of books on their heads, and porters the world over have strong straight backs, developed by carrying loads on their heads.

▷ Stretching your spine up against the weight of gravity makes your meditation pose "firm and comfortable", as Patanjali recommends.

favourite cushion, or spread out a lovely rug. The corner might contain a table holding a candle and flowers, or anything you find soothing and inspiring.

objects of devotion

The things you keep in your meditation corner can be used for the classic technique called *tratak* – or "gazing". This involves sitting erect and motionless while focusing your gaze upon an object.

The point of focus is often a lighted candle. If you practise this form of meditation, check that there are no draughts to move the candle flame, as this can give you a headache. (Epileptics and migraine sufferers should avoid gazing at a flame.) After gazing softly, without staring, for a while, close your eyes and keep the image in your mind's eye. When it fades, gaze at the candle again and repeat the visualization. Your mental image will gradually become firmer and your concentration deeper.

You may like to light a candle before starting meditation practice and blow it out with a "thank you" as a final gesture. A flame is a universal symbol for the presence of the divine, and you may like to develop a greater awareness of this presence dwelling within you and surrounding you.

There are different forms of tratak. A flower can be held and turned around in the hand, as you observe every detail of its beauty and structure. Holding a crystal in your hands and feeling its contours and coolness is another form of tratak – in this case the eyes are closed throughout and the "gazing" is accomplished through the sense of touch. You could equally well choose to gaze at any object that inspires you.

relaxing horizontal stretch

Stretching out on your back is the perfect preparation for meditation. Ten minutes lying stretched out on the floor on your back, with your mind gently but firmly focused on the movement of your breath while your body relaxes, is an instant restorative.

△ Keep alert and warm while you relax on your back. Stretching in this position prepares you for keeping your spine erect – the spine should always be as straight as possible when meditating. While you lie on your back and relax your body, many meditation techniques can be used to keep your mind alert and focused, such as counting your breaths from one to ten and back again, visualizing energy moving through the spine, repeating a mantra, or visualizing a tranquil scene in the country or by the sea. After your relaxation take a few deep breaths, move your fingers and toes, stretch and yawn and sit up very slowly. You are now ready for meditation practice.

Using the Senses

We relate to the world around us by means of our five senses, and these same senses also tell us what we are thinking and how we are feeling. They are the link between the world outside us – which everyone else can experience – and the world inside us that only we can know. By increasing our powers of observation, visualization and imagination, meditation practices help to sharpen our senses. By these means we can actually change how we feel inside ourselves.

Meditation and the five senses

Our senses are the antennae that our minds use to probe the world, both outside and within us, so that we can become aware of what is happening, and what we are doing and thinking. What we are unable to feel, see, hear, taste or smell we can neither conceive of nor describe. Without our five senses we could have no first-hand information about anything and would remain in ignorance, even of our own bodies. Yet their range can pick up only a tiny fraction of what is actually "out there" and "in here" – even when enhanced by modern technology.

We may claim to have a "sixth" sense – or intuition – but this arises from the five physical senses working together. Try thinking about anything without "hearing" yourself thinking about it or "seeing" it in your mind's eye. We can even "feel" in two minds about some issue and "hear" voices arguing the pros and cons in our heads.

CHAKRAS AND THE SENSES

1 Base (*muladhara*): Earth element and sense of smell.

2 Sacral (*svadisthana*): Water element and sense of taste.

3 Navel (*manipura*): Fire element and sense of sight.

4 Heart (*anahata*): Air element and sense of touch.

5 Throat (*vishuddhi*): Ether or Space element and sense of hearing.

pratyahara for focus and awareness

Meditation is a state of expanded awareness, and awareness is simply becoming conscious of specific sensory messages once the general sensory "noise" of everyday experience is switched off.

Pratyahara is the fifth of Patanjali's eight limbs. It is often translated as "withdrawing the senses from their objects", so that we are no longer distracted by what is going on around us. However, if we are fearful or anxious, the nervous system will not allow us to be off guard in this way, even for a moment. This state of anxiety is very stressful and eventually exhausts the body's systems, leading to illness.

△ All that we know about the world – from the scent of a flower to the beating of our own hearts – is conveyed to us through our senses.

Pratyahara is associated with deep relaxation, which is the opposite of being "on guard", and it is possible to relax like this when we feel completely safe and at ease in a protected environment, such as a personal meditation corner at home. In this situation we can let our guard down, but if we switch off all the senses we go to sleep. Instead, the answer is to focus on one sense, or turn the senses inward to practise visualization and witness thoughts as they arise. These techniques prepare us for the state of meditation.

prana mudra: gestures for moving energy through the spine

You can increase your awareness of the energy "highway" that corresponds to the central nervous system by visualizing energy moving up and down the spine and passing through the chakras. Eventually you will perceive these movements as actual rather than imaginary, and can start meditating on the qualities of the chakras. This will deepen your relationship with your senses.

△ **1** Sitting erect and comfortable in a cross-legged position, bring your palms to face your lower abdomen with fingertips just touching. Start to breathe in, feeling that you are drawing vital energy up from the earth through the base of your body into the life chakras in the abdominal area.

△ **2** Continue breathing in as your raise your hands slowly up the front of your body, "drawing" the energy up through the spine and into the love chakras in the heart area.

△ **3** Continue, still breathing in, raising your hands and drawing the energy up through the throat area.

△ **5** Now breathe out slowly as you lean forward to bring your head and joined hands to the floor in an attitude of relaxed and trusting surrender. This is the basic grounding position. Repeat the sequence once or twice more.

△ **4** Finish the breath in by taking your hands up past your face (the area of the light chakras), spreading your arms wide and looking up. This is a joyful, exuberant movement.

Sight, taste and smell

Many traditional meditation techniques are based on focusing with awareness upon one or more of the five senses through practising pratyahara. In Patanjali's system this is the last of the outer, or "active", limbs, before the mind turns "inward".

using sight for meditation

Tratak – gazing at an object such as a candle flame or a flower – is a favourite meditation technique that is common to many traditions. It is a simple but highly effective way to rest a busy mind.

1 Look softly upon your chosen object without staring, blinking or thinking. When you feel the need to close your eyes do so, but keep the image of the object motionless in your "mind's eye". The image will gradually fade and, when it does so, open your eyes and gaze again upon the object. Repeat for a total of about ten minutes.

2 You may find that tears will start to flow as you practise tratak, washing the eyeballs. In ancient India, where clean water was in short supply and the environment was very dusty, tratak was practised as a safe cleansing technique for the eyes. Sometimes tears bring emotions to the surface to "wash away" ancient sorrows – let them flow, as this process can be very healing.

◁ **Bringing the full intensity of the sense of sight to bear on a candle flame is a popular meditative technique. Place the candle at about arm's length, with the flame at eye level. (You should avoid gazing at a candle flame if you are prone to migraines or epilepsy.)**

the sense of sight

Sight is probably our most conscious and developed sense in modern western society. Our environment is constantly lit, so that we can move about and work at any hour, regardless of the natural rhythms of day and night, and we are bombarded by visual messages, ranging from traffic lights or advertising hoardings to television and computer screens. It is hard to find a place that is softly lit and visually soothing unless we create it for ourselves in our own home. Most of us find it easier to picture something with the "mind's eye" than to feel or hear it, so visualization is a popular pratyahara technique.

△ **Gazing at a single flower, focus all your attention on every aspect of its appearance: its intricate form, colour and texture.**

THE CHAKRAS IN COLOUR

In Western healing circles the chakras are often "seen" as the colours of the rainbow, rather than using the intricate traditional Eastern diagrams of energies, known as *yantras*:

- ■ **Base chakra:** a deep fiery red like the embers of a coal fire; it is dull blackish red when unhealthy or stagnating.

- ■ **Sacral chakra:** a glowing orange; drab and brownish when lacking energy

- ■ **Navel chakra:** a bright sunny yellow; tinged green when resentful or envious

- ■ **Heart chakra:** emerald green, or often its complementary colour, rose pink; faded when energy is blocked

- ■ **Throat chakra:** brilliant sapphire blue, especially when inspired or defending the truth

- ■ **Brow chakra:** royal purple or amethyst, sometimes indigo (containing the three primary colours of red, yellow and blue)

- ■ **Crown chakra:** brilliant white or pale lilac, radiating as a beacon of light

As you breathe slowly up and down through your chakras, what colours do you "see" them? Remember to ground yourself in prana mudra after you finish this visualization.

△ Focus on your sense of taste by experiencing pure flavours, in this case lemon-flavoured water, with total attention.

the senses of taste and smell

Taste and smell are closely linked, each affecting the other extremely powerfully. They are also our most primitive senses, associated with the reptilian brain and the two lowest chakras, and they are essential for our survival. The most fleeting fragrances have the power to release emotions and memories, and in many religious traditions, aromatics such as incense are used to elevate the spirit or to induce altered states of consciousness. Taste and smell can be included in your meditation by burning incense or fragrant oils and by eating or drinking as an exercise in awareness.

VISUALIZING THE GUNAS

It is easy to understand nature's three "strands" in visual terms and to create our own imagery:

- **Tamas** (inertia, depression, obstruction) looks dull and dark, like an immovable rock or a stagnant murky pond. Everything appears gloomy when we are feeling unhappy.

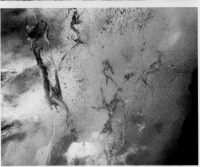

- **Rajas** (movement, passion, obsession, anger) looks hot and fierce, like a devouring and uncontrolled fire. We say that we "see red" when in a fury.

- **Sattva** (balance, harmony, peace) looks bright and light, like polished silver or gold. We can see love "shining" in someone's face and angels are often represented dressed in gleaming white robes.

△ Incense is a traditional aid to meditation. Burn it in your meditation corner to purify the air and focus your sense of smell.

Do any of these images correspond to how you are feeling right now? The gunas are intermingled in every aspect of nature, like a plaited rope, but one of them usually predominates. The only guna suitable for meditation practice is sattva, as neither of the other two makes us feel safe and relaxed.

Hearing and touch

Pratyahara involves a gathering in of the thoughts by consciously detaching the mind from all the fleeting sensations presented to it by the five senses, which are constantly bombarded by all the distractions of the outside world.

the sense of hearing

We are so beset by noise pollution in modern Western society that our sense of hearing often becomes blunted by the cacophony, yet this sense can take us more quickly and also deeper into meditation than any of the others once we have learned to really listen intently but in a completely relaxed manner. One of the classical treatises on hatha yoga (the *Hatha Yoga Pradipika*) leads the student through all the hatha practices – "for the sole purpose of attaining the yoga of meditation" – until the object of meditation can be heard within.

inner sound

What you can hear, once you know how to listen, is the inner vibration or sound, which is called *nada*. This sound is described as having several levels of subtlety. Moving from the grosser sounds to the most subtle,

△ To draw the deep resonant sound from a Tibetan singing bowl, a wooden wand is held very firmly against the side of the bowl as it is stroked around the rim.

◁ At its most resonant level, the inner sound, or nada, is compared with the crashing of waves in the ocean.

the levels are likened to "the ocean... [thunder]clouds, kettledrum... conch [a seashell that can be blown into to create a sound], gong and horn... tinkling of bells, flute, vina [a stringed instrument] and humming of bees".

Anyone who has learnt to relax, still the chattering mind and really listen will be able to hear nada. It is often heard at first as a

◁ Complicated rhythms can be created by a drummer, but keeping time can be as simple or as complex as you wish. Clapping is an excellent and simple way to sustain a rhythm, either alone or in a group.

high-pitched vibrational hum, such as you might hear when standing beneath overhead power cables. Once you can hear nada you should listen for the more subtle levels of sound behind the one that is apparent.

the primordial sound

Many spiritual traditions claim that creation began with sound. St John's gospel opens with the statement: "In the beginning was the Word," and this primordial word is clearly a sound caused, like all sounds, by a vibration. The same claim is made in the *Mandukya Upanishad*, one of the philosophical and mystical treatises that form part of the Vedas: "Whatever has been, is or shall be is OM and whatever transcends time is also OM." OM is known as the *pranava* or primordial sound and is placed at the beginning of most mantras, as well as being the source of every mantra. It is the sacred sound or vibration that gave rise to the universe as we know it. Therefore the reverent chanting of OM takes us back to our creator or source, God or Brahman. Nada is the sound of the divine within us.

developing your ability to listen

An effective pratyahara technique is to sit quietly and focus upon your sense of hearing without involving any movement of the mind. Start by picking up the most obvious sounds, such as a car in the street or a dog barking somewhere. Listen to these sounds, simply becoming aware of them without making any mental comment such as "That is a dog's bark," or framing any judgement or description of the sound, such

as "ugly" or "loud". Gradually listen for more subtle sounds, such as your own breathing, heartbeat or digestion – still without the addition of any mental comments. Hear your own thoughts without making any comment upon them. Eventually, when you have learned how to listen impartially to whatever sounds you are picking up, you will hear nada.

making your own sounds

Having learned to hear sounds impartially, you can learn to produce sounds without any of the "mental baggage" that usually accompanies attempts to create tuneful noises such as singing or playing musical instruments. You can chant a simple mantra, stroke a Tibetan singing bowl with a wooden wand, sing a scale up and down through an octave, create rhythm on a drum, all without embarrassment or stress, whether you are alone or in company. Both listening to and creating sounds are wonderfully relaxing practices that can quickly take you into the meditative state.

the sense of touch

Every emotional response is a matter of "feeling", involving some aspect of the physical sense of touch. Feeling safe is like being held by loving hands or feeling the presence of friends around you. Feeling inspired or uplifted creates a tangible feeling of inner lightness and expansion. You can also feel "in touch" with your body – whether you are hot or cold, comfortable or in pain, still or moving.

Most of these sensations remain below consciousness unless we need to notice them. In our daily lives, we are unaware of the muscles that keep us standing upright until we trip and are in danger of falling, or of our breathing cycles until we run too fast and feel out of breath. Learning to consciously feel safe and relaxed while becoming more focused and aware is a wonderful antidote to stress.

△ Really feeling the shape, weight, coolness and texture of an object such as a crystal is a valuable meditative practice.

SHARING A SENSE OF TOUCH
Massage is an excellent way to explore and enhance your sense of touch – whether as "giver" or "receiver". You do not need to be an expert. Simply remember that your hands are extensions of your heart chakra, ask your partner how they feel and tune in to their responses. It helps communication to synchronize your breathing with your partner; press down as they breathe out and relax, lightening your touch on the breath in.

△ Giving or receiving massage allows both of you to focus on the sense of touch.

Combining the senses

△ **A meditation table can cater for all the senses:** include a flower to look at; a lemon and some sprigs of an aromatic herb such as basil for smell and taste; essential oils in a burner to create fragrance conducive to meditation; a crystal to look at and touch; and a mala to handle as you hear yourself repeating a mantra.

the dominant sense

People often have a bias toward one of the five senses. The sense of sight is probably dominant for most people in modern Western society, though some people rely more upon hearing or touch than upon sight, and the other senses may be far more important to us than we realize.

It is impossible to write anything without hearing the words spoken in our own mind, or to move around without being aware through the sense of touch of the body's relationship with everything around it. The senses of taste and smell are far more active than we may imagine. Therefore combining the focusing of several senses in meditation practice is likely to be more effective than concentrating on just one.

combining sensory tools to deepen meditation

Start with simple techniques that use only one sense until you have learned to stay focused on it for several minutes at a time. Then gradually increase the complexity of the exercise and find what works best for you and holds your attention longest.

Practise regularly a simple technique such as feeling the movement of your breath within your body (which relies on your sense of touch). This technique may eventually become so familiar that your mind can wander even while you are doing it, making focusing difficult. When this happens you can change to a different technique – perhaps alternate nostril breathing with counting (combining the senses of touch and sound). Then explore "seeing" or "feeling" prana, or energy, as light or warmth or tingling as you breathe. Direct this prana mentally as you breathe in and take it to a specific place within your body on the breath out (combining the senses of sight and touch).

These sensory tools are deceptively simple to use in order to reach the meditative state, yet they can have profound

Sensory perception is a mental activity. The brain turns the constant input of nervous impulses from the body into touch, sight, hearing, taste and smell so as to make internal sense of the external world. We do not actually know what lies outside our brain, only what it tells us is there as it translates the impressions picked up by the sensory nerve endings.

Most of what our senses pick up is filtered out from our conscious awareness. For instance, while we are reading a book that is engrossing our interest, we may not notice other people moving about around us. All kinds of forces exist that we cannot sense, such as the cosmic rays called neutrinos that pass straight through our "solid" bodies and our planet.

△ When you become absorbed in a book your brain is able to ignore outside distractions even though all your senses are still picking up all the signals from them.

▽ While you are watching yourself writing, and feeling your hand steering the pen, you are also hearing the words inside your head.

effects over time. Just taking three deep breaths – if that has become your trigger – can immediately lift you out of a state of stress and into inner silence. The art is to combine several tools so as to maintain mental awareness and focus, and avoid slipping into daydreaming.

All meditation practices use the natural senses, usually touch, sight or sound and often a combination of these. You can learn to sharpen all your senses, one at a time, and then to switch off your perception of the outer world at will in order to create an inner world. Visualization is the technique of creating your own reality. "As we think, so we become", so think happy and relaxed thoughts, flowing with life-light-love. Your external world will reflect the attitudes that you project on to it from within.

MALA AND MANTRA

Fingering a mala (a string of traditional meditation beads) while chanting a mantra is a classic example of a meditative technique that combines the senses. Two senses are being used here: the sense of hearing as you listen to yourself repeating the mantra (either chanting it out loud or saying it in your mind) and the sense of touch as you pass the mala through your fingers to clock up the repetitions of the mantra.

Sit erect and relaxed in the safe environment of your meditation corner. Favourite mantras are "OM", "Peace and goodwill", "OM shanti shanti shanti" (*shanti* means "peace") or any short phrase that promotes healing and joy. Really feel the presence of the beads as you finger them gently but decisively.

△ The mala is held in the right hand, and the positions of the fingers used to count the repetitions are symbolic: the thumb (cosmic consciousness) and the middle finger (sattva guna) move the beads, while the first finger (ego/personality consciousness) is kept well away from the action.

The art of visualization

Visualization is a technique that brings the senses into full play, and enables us to build up a happy inner world. Relaxed visualization is a tool used in many different types of therapies. Its aim is to help us change our perception of the world by changing the way we feel inside ourselves. It can be done lying down or reclining just as well as sitting in an upright meditation pose. This means that we can help ourselves to feel better when we are tired and depleted, or ill in bed, or needing to create a calm and relaxed state to prepare for a peaceful night's sleep.

choosing an affirmation

You can use your relaxation time for your own greatest long-term benefit by using affirmations to create lasting change. The first step is to decide on an affirmation or resolve, known as a *sankalpa*, to repeat when you are in a state of deep relaxation.

You need to ask yourself what positive changes in your behaviour (life), perception (light) or attitude (love) would make you more like the person you would wish to be. The answer requires reflection and an honest appraisal of your personal qualities. Having decided on your sankalpa, you can set about creating a suitable visualization by using your imagination and all five senses to become fully present in a place of your choice where you feel naturally safe and relaxed. Once this scene is set you can go

△ **For relaxation adopt a comfortable position lying on your back with your knees raised and feet flat on the floor. A cushion under your head keeps your neck from contracting at the back.**

▽ **Once you are deeply relaxed, focus your imagination and all your senses on being present in the place you want to be.**

deeper and reinforce the changes in attitude, outlook and purpose that you have already decided to adopt. The unconscious mind is happy to respond to the suggestions put to it by the conscious mind, provided your nervous system is in a thoroughly relaxed and trusting state and that you express your intention in the following ways:

- Phrase your affirmation as clearly and as briefly as possible, with no "ifs" and "buts", descriptions or qualifiers.

CREATIVE IMAGINING

It has been said that nothing can be imagined that we have not already experienced – either at first or second hand. We have an almost infinite variety of memories to choose from. Our life happens in our heads, so we should create as harmonious an inner world as we possibly can. There is no need to put up with a haphazard and chaotic inner world once you know how to change it. The choice is yours and meditation techniques are the tools.

- Mention just one change. When that change has occurred you can replace your sankalpa because it will have become redundant.
- Describe the change you wish for in the present tense, such as "I am…[happy, healthy, confident, successful at…, or forgiving of…]" or, "I am becoming more and more…day by day." The unconscious mind lives only in the present and ignores the past or future. Tomorrow never comes and is of no interest to it.
- Express your sankalpa in positive terms only, for the unconscious mind becomes confused by negative words such as "not" and "never".
- Avoid any words like "try" or "work at" or "difficult" because they immediately put the nervous system on guard and undo all the good relaxation you have achieved up to now.
- Repeat your sankalpa three times slowly and decisively, so that your unconscious mind knows you mean business. In this way you are programming it to carry out your intentions all the time – even when the conscious mind is busy with other things. This is why the sankalpa has such a powerful effect.

VISUALIZING A BEACH SCENE

You have become deeply relaxed, perhaps after some stretching and deep breathing exercises. Sit or lie down in a comfortable position and start to imagine yourself reclining on a beautiful beach. You are lying on soft sand near the water's edge on a pleasant sunny day. Use all your senses to appreciate all the details of the scene, so that you experience it fully.

You can feel the texture and dampness of the sand beneath you, dig your toes into it and let it run through your fingers. Look at the scenery around you, the deep blue of the sea and sky, the pale sand, the distant horizon, a few fluffy white clouds, seagulls flying overhead. You can hear the seagulls calling, the wavelets lapping across the sand and the sound of a gentle breeze moving the leaves of the trees behind you. You can smell the salt air and taste it on your

△ The beauty, warmth and peace of a tropical beach make it pleasing to all the senses, so it is an ideal subject for a visualization to help you create your happy inner world.

▷ The more detailed your visualization the more completely you will be able to experience the scene. Taste and feel the coolness of an iced drink on a hot day.

lips. What else can you feel, see and hear? Perhaps the air caressing your body, the intricate patterns of individual grains of sand and tiny shells, the sound of children laughing in the distance. Can you smell the sea, taste a half-eaten peach, feel the welcome coolness of the wind lifting your hair?

When you have built up all the details of this lovely scene, stay in it for a while feeling peaceful and contented, grateful and relaxed. The whole purpose of this visualization is to bring you to this inner place where you know that "all is well", now and always. Before you decide to leave the beach repeat your sankalpa (the affirmation or resolve you have already decided upon) slowly and clearly three times. Then gradually let the whole scene dissolve, knowing that it is always there for you to return to, no matter what is going on in the external world.

◁ Feel the sand between your toes and visualize the soft sheen of seashells.

Visualizations while in deep relaxation are enjoyable and can reveal unexpected insights. They prepare for more structured traditional meditations.

The visualization described opposite takes you on a journey that starts with your everyday awareness and leads to a higher level of consciousness, as you walk slowly through the countryside and up a hill to your goal before returning more quickly by the same route. The Buddhist walking meditation, a practice in which the action of walking is itself the focus of awareness, can be a helpful preparation for your imaginary walk through the chakra fields. Remember to perform a grounding ritual at the end of your visualization to avoid feeling "spaced out" afterwards.

TELLING THE STORY

You may wish to make a tape of the visualization described opposite so that your voice guides you gently through it, with frequent pauses to build up the scene in your mind. Or get a friend to read it aloud to you. It should take about 20 minutes.

walking meditation

This popular Buddhist meditation combines the senses of touch, sound and sight. Walking in slow motion requires focus and concentration. Synchronize your breathing and mantra repetitions with your steps.

△ **1** Stand tall with your mala held in front of you at heart level. Very slowly raise one foot and step forward on to it, bending your back knee. As you step forward, keep your weight distributed evenly between both feet.

△ **2** Take your whole weight on to your front foot, lifting your back foot and standing as tall as you can. Gaze straight ahead all the time. Repeat the movements, saying your mantra with each step.

A WALK THROUGH THE CHAKRA FIELDS

Relax deeply, feeling your senses becoming very alert so that you notice every detail of your imaginary surroundings.

 Start by walking along a short lane that takes you to a stile giving access to a meadow. A sea of red flowers – perhaps poppies – grow in this field. They represent the vitality and growth of the base chakra. A footpath leads you gently uphill across this field to another stile. Follow this path, absorbing the vibrant redness, feeling the solid ground beneath you and the movement of your legs and feet as you walk. Inhale the natural earthy smell of living, growing plants.

 The next stile takes you into a grove of orange trees laden with ripe fruit, representing the sensuality of the sacral chakra. Enjoy the abundance of nature and its glorious power to reproduce and sustain life. Eat some of the fruit, letting the delicious juices flow in your mouth. Dance your way along the path to the next stile.

△ The sunflower's seeds store up the sun's energy, as the navel chakra stores our life force.

 This leads you into a field of golden sunflowers, representing the light and heat of the navel chakra, which is often called the solar centre. Here we store our reserves of energy, or prana – just as the seeds of the sunflowers store the energy of life. Feast your eyes on the gold around you and let your skin soak up the warmth from the sun. Feel confident that your reserves of energy will always support whatever you set out to accomplish. At the end of the field is a gate in a wall.

 This gate opens into a formal walled garden with a path that takes you under a long archway festooned with climbing roses in every shade of pink, luminous against their glossy green leaves and exuding heavenly scents. This beautiful garden represents your heart chakra, with its atmosphere of peace and joy. You touch the velvety petals and the roses lean down to share their beauty with you, inviting you to pick them. You take just one to keep as your constant companion, before passing through the gate at the end of the garden.

 You find yourself on high ground under a wide blue sky across which birds are flying and calling to each other. The sky is reflected in pools of blue water from melting snows, and vivid blue gentians open their faces to the warm sun. This scene represents the throat chakra and the energies of pure space and sound. You hear your name being called and walk trustingly toward a high pass ahead of you.

△ Notice every detail of the lush growth that fringes your path on your walk.

 Someone comes to meet you, offering to guide you onward and representing your own higher wisdom, found in your brow chakra. This chakra is often called the third eye: the "all-seeing eye" of the higher mind that unites the two hemispheres of the brain – logical intellect and creative imagination – to create insight. Your guide may tell you something or give you something to ponder upon later, before leading you over the pass.

 Beyond is a grassy glade surrounded by trees. In the centre is a small white building – clearly a very special and spiritual place – that represents your crown chakra. Your guide gestures to you to enter alone, which you do very respectfully. There you sit and repeat your sankalpa, slowly and clearly, three times. You remain in this place, absorbing its spiritual energies, until you feel it is time to return to everyday awareness. You say "thank you" before rising and leaving to walk slowly back the way you have come, knowing that you can return here whenever you wish.

Back in the lane where you started your journey you become aware once more of your physical body. Take a few deep breaths, move your fingers and toes, yawn and stretch. Perform your grounding ritual to end your session, then get up slowly.

△ The endless blue sky represents the throat chakra, whose element is ether, or space.

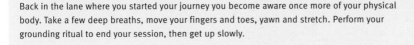

Everyday
Meditation

The ancient wisdom of both West and East offers tools to help us live our lives in joy and peace, and can provide simple reasons to explain why and how people behave in the ways they do – so that we can better understand, accept and forgive ourselves and other people. When meditation becomes part of daily life, it can help us to improve the quality of all our interactions with the world around us.

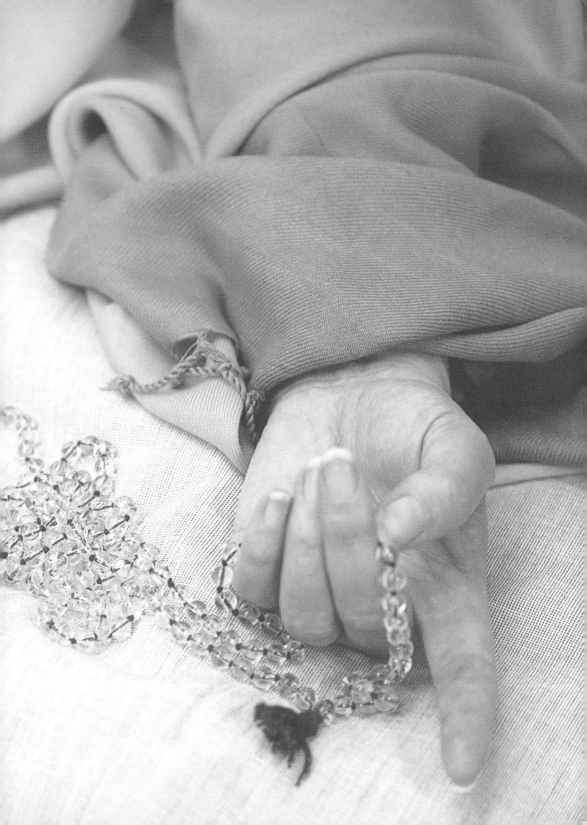

Meditation in daily life

Many people think of the meditative state as being rather "otherworldly", something that they can only achieve if they divorce themselves from daily life. Although regular meditation practice requires that we set time aside to turn the attention inward, it can also be woven into daily life. We can turn mundane chores into a form of meditation by practising "mindfulness" – focusing all our thoughts on them; we can experience a sense of spiritual enlightenment from appreciating the beauty of everything around us; we can use meditative practices when trying to engage with and understand our emotions; and we can introduce meditative elements into the ways in which we relate to others.

▷ **By focusing all your awareness on everyday activities such as eating, you can turn them into a form of meditation.**

key elements

There are many ways in which you can bring meditation into every aspect of your day-to-day life:

- Focus your mind and body entirely on what you are doing at this moment, letting distractions wash around you.

- Live in the present moment as much as you can.
- Try to perceive the beauty and worth in everything (and everyone) around you, and in everything you do, no matter how mundane the task.

- Learn to use your senses to the full.
- Develop self-awareness, and work with the interplay between your emotional and physical self – noticing how certain breathing practices and positions affect your mental state, for example.

WORKING WITH YOUR FEELINGS

The following traditional technique, based on experiencing "opposites", allows you to become impartially aware of your feelings (many of which are usually below consciousness):

- Relax deeply – sitting, reclining or lying on your back.
- Imagine various "pairs of opposites" and notice the physical sensations that arise.
- Start with pairs that have little or no positive/negative emotional associations – such as hot/cold, hard/soft, light/dark – and

observe how you feel in your body while remaining deeply relaxed.

- Move on to a more emotionally challenging pair, starting with the positive side, and observe what feelings are evoked: birth/death, spacious/confined, happy/sad, delighted/angry and welcome/excluded are some examples.
- Still deeply relaxed, observe what feelings arise in your body as you contemplate the negative half of the pair – so that you can recognize and identify them from

now on and understand what "pushes your buttons" and how you feel out of sorts when your emotions are negative. You can then take appropriate action to make you feel better and defuse tension in and around you.

- Repeat the positive half of the pair before moving on to the next pair of opposites.
- End with your sankalpa and some gentle deep breathing before coming out of relaxation with a grounding ritual.

RELATING TO OTHERS

This Buddhist "loving kindness" meditation helps you to relate better to those around you. Breathe in universal love and kindness to help and support yourself, then breathe it out, directing it to a specific person or group. Repeat this meditation often, until it becomes second nature both to receive and to give loving kindness. Make it part of your daily life: any part of it can be used in any situation to promote peace and harmony.

- Relax deeply in a seated position with your spine erect.
- Breathe in, drawing "loving kindness" from the universe into yourself.
- Breathe out, directing that loving kindness with gratitude toward a particular person, or to all those who have taught you (given you light in many ways). Breathe more loving kindness into yourself.
- Breathe out, directing loving kindness with gratitude toward a particular

person or to all those who have nurtured and nourished you (given you life in many forms). Breathe in...
- Breathe out, directing loving kindness with blessings toward a person or people you love dearly. Breathe in...
- Breathe out, directing loving kindness with blessings toward acquaintances, neighbours, people you work with. Breathe in...
- Breathe out, directing loving kindness with forgiveness to people who annoy or obstruct you, who are unkind or dismissive. Breathe in...
- Breathe out, directing loving kindness with forgiveness to anyone who has ever hurt or injured you in any way. Breathe in...
- Breathe out, radiating the prayer, "May all people everywhere be happy." Breathe in and give thanks for all the loving kindness you receive. Pause before coming out of your meditation and grounding yourself with a ritual.

△ The traditional Indian greeting "Namaste", spoken with a bow while bringing the hands together at the heart chakra, acknowledges the presence of the divine in the heart of each person, conveying the sense that everyone is part of the unity of creation.

how are you feeling?

As a way of linking the physical and non-physical, it is important to get into the habit of noticing consciously what your senses are telling your mind. This makes it much easier to monitor your emotions as they arise, because you can feel them through your senses. In fact, there is no other way to feel how you are "feeling". For every emotion there is a corresponding physical sensation: we "see red" when angry, our legs "turn to jelly" when we are frightened, sadness makes the heart "ache" or we are "in the dark" when confused.

Once you learn to recognize how you are actually feeling you can avoid reacting negatively to everyday situations. Whenever you notice a negative feeling arising, pause for an instant (the proverbial "counting to ten"), relax and visualize the positive, opposite feeling. You can then respond in a positive manner instead, bringing what you have learned through the regular practice of meditation into your daily life.

▷ Use the time you spend in the bath or shower each day to relax and enjoy the present moment.

◁ When you take a walk among plants and trees, focus your whole mind and all your senses on the experience, noticing the beauty of everything you pass along your path. Plants teach us how to "just be".

Renounce and enjoy

The idea of "renounce and enjoy" comes from a teaching found in the *Isha Upanishad* and reflects another meditative concept that we can bring into our daily lives. This teaching states:

All this, whatsoever moves in this Universe, is indwelled by Isha: therefore, through renunciation do thou enjoy, and do not covet anybody's wealth.

The Upanishads share with Patanjali a belief in the philosophy of absolute unity, with the divine presence of sat-chit-ananda – life-light-love – directing and managing our world. According to this belief, everything is part of the indivisible whole that we simply breathe in and out like air.

Every day, we are constantly receiving life, light and love. We are nourished by them, and should then let them go as easily as they came. Our mistake is to try to grasp for ourselves what cannot be owned by anyone and then get stressed by our own greed and lack of trust in the eternal supply.

△ A home environment that is calm and harmonious, with clean, simple lines and clear surfaces, helps to promote an uncluttered mind. It is easy to become weighed down by the need to accumulate possessions, so that we fail to value all the good things that are already part of our lives.

LIFE-LIGHT-LOVE MANTRA
Repeating this mantra, taken from the *Isha Upanishad*, will help you to glimpse the truth of divine life-light-love and absolute unity:
That [eternal life-light-love] is full; this [the changing world] is full.
From full, the full is taken; the full has come.
If you take out full from the full, the full alone remains.

"He who bends to himself a Joy
Doth the winged thing destroy;
But he who kisses the joy as it flies
Lives in Eternity's sunrise."
William Blake, 1757-1827

what should we renounce?

"Renunciation" does not mean giving up everything that is enjoyable in life. It does not mean parting with all our possessions, or giving up actual objects or pastimes that we may enjoy, but giving up our attachment to all these things. As has often been said, it is not money, nor even the pleasant things it can buy, but "the love of money" – our attachment to it – that is the problem.

The traditional story of the prince and the merchant illustrates the point of renunciation very well. You might like to use it regularly as a basis for visualizations or meditations that will help you to bring this quality into your life. You could repeat a section of it over and over as a meditative mantra, anywhere and at any time.

△ For Zen Buddhists, the creation of a garden such as this is seen as an active form of meditation, in which the large is experienced in the small, and the meaning of the whole world encapsulated in a grain of sand. Respect for nature and a sense of connectedness with natural cycles are basic tenets of Zen Buddhism.

The Story of the Prince and the Merchant

There was once a Hindu prince who became friendly with a merchant. The prince admired the merchant's knowledge and love of beautiful objects and the way he conducted his business, so he asked if he could accompany him on a buying trip.

The two set out together and came to another merchant's emporium. Entering the dimness of this cave of treasures, the merchant looked around and then enquired the price of a few articles. The owner laughed and said: "I know what you are after! You have seen the bejewelled box that makes up the set you have been collecting for years," and he quoted an astronomical price. The merchant replied, "Yes, I have seen it and I will give you a fair price and no more." When the owner refused to reduce his price the merchant beckoned to the prince and they left and continued along the dusty road.

The prince remonstrated, "But you can't let it go!" The merchant smiled, "Oh no! I intend to buy it." Sure enough, a few moments later the owner of the emporium came panting up to them, box in hand. "Here," he said, "have

▽ The bonfire visualized by the merchant destroys his possessions but cannot rob him of his experience of them.

△ We may treasure our possessions, but the idea of renunciation means that we are also happy to let them go.

it – it completes your set and is not worth much on its own. Name your price." The two merchants struck a deal and the prince was most impressed.

The prince asked to try his skill at the next suitable place but things did not go so well for him. He found a dagger that he knew had been made for his family, because of its distinctive shape and design. He wanted it very much, but when he refused to pay the inflated price being asked and left the shop, the owner did not pursue him. "What have I done wrong?" he asked his friend, who replied, "When I left the box behind I completely let go of it in my mind and the seller sensed this. When you left the dagger behind, you kept on wanting it and the seller knows you will return and pay whatever price he asks."

The prince asked for the secret of true renunciation and the merchant told him: "Each night before I sleep I visualize a bonfire. I pile on it everything I own and watch it all burn to ashes. Then I pile on everything I care about – my friends, wife, children and finally myself – and watch it all burn away. Then I give thanks for what I have enjoyed that day and sleep soundly. In the morning I find that all that I value has been returned to me and I thank the Lord for his goodness. This is the secret of my happiness and my success – I practise both enjoying and letting go with gratitude."

Getting to know yourself

AVOIDING OVER-ATTACHMENT

It is a mistake to become too attached to any one of the three gunas – even the bright and beautiful sattva guna. The gunas are strands of nature, which is described as energy in flux, ever-changing and therefore never real. Traditional prayers are often chanted for dissolving our attachment to nature and the gunas, in order to focus on the eternal reality of consciousness (or spirit). The following mantras (translated from the Sanskrit) are frequently used for group and private meditation:

*"Lead us from the unreal to
    the real,
From darkness to light
And from death to immortality."*

*"...May Shiva [supreme
consciousness] liberate all beings.
May he liberate us from death [the
impermanence of nature and the
gunas] for the sake of immortality
[living in the eternal now] even as
the ripe cucumber drops naturally
from the vine [of attachments]."*

▽ **We seek freedom from attachment rather like a ripe cucumber falling from the vine.**

Everyone can benefit from getting into the habit of recognizing the various forces that make us think, feel and behave as we do in our daily lives. It is helpful to consider these forces working within us in terms of the chakras, koshas and gunas. Even when we are alone, our behaviour, thoughts and attitudes reflect the interactions between the koshas that are constantly taking place within the chakras.

correcting imbalances

Describing these inner processes in terms of the three gunas can help us to become aware of any imbalances. The three strands of the gunas are interwoven at every level: at the physical (anna maya kosha) and energetic (prana maya kosha) levels, the instinctive mental (mano maya kosha) and intellectual (vijnana maya kosha) levels,

△ **Meditation allows you to quieten the constant background chatter of your thoughts to contemplate things clearly and impartially, fostering greater self-knowledge.**

and also at the level of feeling and purpose (ananda maya kosha).

We cannot escape the qualities of tamas, rajas and sattva, but through meditation we can learn to influence which one is dominant. In tamas we are stuck fast, going nowhere and achieving nothing. We need the desire and energy of rajas to get things moving, but too much makes us the slaves of passion. A balance of tamas and rajas – of rest and exertion – brings sattva, in which peace and balance can predominate. This is the state required for meditation: the preliminary practices such as stretching and breathing are designed to achieve and maintain sattva, in which a

balanced nervous system can respond appropriately to each moment as it arises.

Meditation allows us to stand back and observe ourselves impartially, as witnesses who are prepared to recognize and accept what we find, reflect upon it and then create change. We can then restore inner harmony whenever we feel it slipping from us, and live in the harmonious state of being that Patanjali described:

*"...the qualities of the heart are cultivated:
friendliness towards the joyful,
compassion towards the suffering,
happiness towards the pure
and impartiality towards the impure."
(A. Shearer's translation of the Sutras, Ch 1)*

This is what is known to Buddhists as the "practice of the four virtues".

Lord Krishna's dance – developing harmony and balance

Lord Krishna is the Hindu lord of love and the embodiment of divine beauty and joy. He expresses love's eternal flow through movement. The air moves through his reed flute to create enchanting music, and his body moves in joyful dance. This is an active balancing meditation that helps to bring about physical and mental harmony.

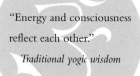

"Energy and consciousness reflect each other."

Traditional yogic wisdom

△ **1** Stand tall on your left leg, and slowly raise your right leg up and across to the left. Then turn your trunk to the right, raising both your arms to the right as if you are holding and playing a flute. "Hear" the music you are playing while "feeling" Krishna's lightness and joy.

△ **2** Lower your right foot gracefully to the floor, stepping across the left, and turn to face straight ahead, keeping your arms raised. Transfer your weight to your right foot and raise your left leg to repeat the dancing step, turning your body to the left.

CHART YOUR STATE OF BEING

Remember that a degree of tamas and rajas is necessary in life – it is only unhealthy if one of these states dominates. We progress from tamas through rajas to the balanced state of sattva.

TAMAS	RAJAS	SATTVA
The quality of inertia in nature, tamas is a form of poverty and stagnation that can make us feel trapped and deprived. It constricts the flow of life-light-love, preventing us from experiencing and sharing natural spontaneity, inspiration and joy. It saps our energy, making us build emotional walls around ourselves.	Here there is too much of everything – especially passion, spreading out of control like a forest fire. Rajas makes us restless and full of unsatisfied desire; we become aggressive and insensitive to the needs and feelings of others. When rajas is dominant we see other people only as objects that are there to be exploited and manipulated.	The quality of balance or harmony in nature, sattva makes tamas and rajas become complementary and positive rather than destructive, creating light to dissolve both darkness and passion. The sattva guna is calm, pure and kind, but it is still part of the changing pattern of nature rather than unchanging consciousness or spirit.
Stuck in timetables and routine	Self-centred impatience and disregard	Spontaneity and co-operation
Ignorance and prejudice	Contempt for tradition, risk-taking	Understanding and respect
Timidity, fear, victim mentality	Self-confidence, arrogance, aggression	Trust and willingness to share
Dependency on other people	Ambition, wilfulness, domination	Self-reliance and inner guidance
Low energy, self-neglect, poor diet	Greed, drive, eventual burnout	Healthy balanced lifestyle
Illness, helplessness, pain	Determination to survive, lust for life	Acceptance and living life fully
Grief, regrets, sadness	Concentration on the future	Living joyfully in the now
Hopelessness	Feverish desire	Faith in the process and divine plan
Poverty	Determination to succeed no matter what	Content with "enough" and inner joy

Energetic exercise as meditation

If you are bound up in a demanding working life it is easy to feel that you have no time to spare for relaxation or physical exercise. But trying to maintain a high level of mental activity throughout your waking hours soon becomes counter-productive, leading to stress, exhaustion and illness.

A regular exercise routine not only helps to keep the physical body fit and healthy, but also contributes to a balanced lifestyle, helping you to live a busy life with the minimum of stress. Vigorous exercise produces a natural feeling of wellbeing, even euphoria, because it stimulates the release of endorphins, the body's own painkillers, in the brain, making you feel good and releasing mental tension. When you are feeling tamasic – tired and

◁ **Building exercise into your daily routine helps you to achieve a healthy balance between work, rest and exertion, raising your energy levels.**

sluggish – vigorous exercise may seem a daunting prospect, but its rajasic nature can promote the balanced state of sattva if it becomes a regular part of your daily life.

This feeling of inner balance leads to meditation in action – while travelling, at work, at home, at play and in all relationships. Affection, openness, focus and witnessing become your predominant attitudes and frustration, irritability and mood swings are far less frequent.

exercise for relaxation

Energetic exercises, such as the examples shown on these pages, loosen contracted muscles, unwinding stress and unblocking the flow of energy in the body. Whether you choose yoga, dancing, swimming, jogging, go to the gym or play a team sport, the release of tension brought about by exercise allows you to relax fully afterwards, in preparation for the meditative state.

developing spatial awareness

If you practise yoga, a real understanding of the subtleties of the classical poses will help to develop your spiritual and physical awareness, which are vital for successful meditation. Insight can be gained by trying them out in different ways, as with the Dog pose shown here, a vigorous pose that gets the energy flowing.

△ **1** The Dog pose lying down: in this position, gravity presses your spine flat against the floor so that it is elongated and the chest is opened as you stretch your arms over your head, maintaining contact with the floor from shoulders to fingertips. Your legs are straight and exactly vertical, at right angles to the spine and with heels pushed to the ceiling. Notice where you are stretching and opening the body, and feel which muscles are working.

△ **2** The Dog pose from standing: the classical pose is more vigorous, as you are pushing upward against gravity with your arms and legs. Make exactly the same right-angled shape with your body and maintain the feeling of the flat elongated spine and open chest that you experienced when lying down. Experimenting by inverting the pose will have made you far more aware of what it involves.

cross-crawl exercise

This is a series of vigorous dancelike movements that "wakes up" the brain as well as the body by requiring you to move in an unaccustomed way that requires conscious thought. When you always make certain movements in the same way, you develop neural "habit pathways". This kind of exercise is designed to challenge you to adapt to doing things differently. Similar well-known exercises include the tricks of patting your head with one hand while rubbing your abdomen in circles with the other, or making circles with one arm to a count of three and simultaneously circling the other arm to a count of four.

△ **1** Marching vigorously on the spot, raise your right thigh and left upper arm parallel to the floor for several beats.

△ **2** Without missing a beat, change to raising your right thigh and right upper arm together, followed by your left thigh and left upper arm. Continue marching on the spot for the same number of beats, then change smoothly back to 1 and repeat.

ball of energy

This is a moving visualization that increases spontaneity and flexibility, and makes a good warm-up before vigorous exercise. It engages all the chakras, building firm yet springy strength in the life chakras (abdomen, legs and feet), openness and expansiveness and free expression in the love chakras (chest and neck) and focus and imagination in the light chakras (skull).

△ **1** Stand with the knees loose and springy, the spine stretched up out of the pelvis and the chest open. Start creating an imaginary "ball of energy" between your palms by pushing them lightly against resistance in a kneading motion. They will naturally find the right distance apart after a few moments as you begin to feel the energy passing between them.

△ **2** Toss the ball of energy up in the air and catch it again, stretching loosely and keeping your knees springy. Stay grounded by keeping your feet firmly in contact with the floor. Do not move them.

△ **3** Take the ball of energy to the side in a sweeping circle, then down, to the front and up the other side in a series of sweeping stretches of the upper body. Keep focused on it and enjoy playing with it. Feel the groundedness of your lower body contrasting with the freedom of your upper body and the spontaneity of your movements.

Repetitive tasks as meditation

Performing simple repetitive tasks can become an excellent form of meditation. Such tasks can be very soothing – it all depends upon your attitude. If you are feeling relaxed and in a sattvic frame of mind you can enjoy focusing upon the gentle rhythms of going for a walk, chopping vegetables, filing at the office, knitting, sewing, weeding the garden – even vacuuming the house or doing the washing up. If, on the other hand, you are feeling tamasic – tired and bored – such tasks seem like drudgery and make you feel trapped. In a rajasic mood you may feel impatient and frustrated and your mind will wander as you daydream about doing something or being somewhere more exciting.

mindfulness

By giving all your attention to a simple repetitive task you become aware of every detail of what you are doing, living fully in the present and bringing all your senses to bear on the experience. In this relaxed state of awareness, the mind simply witnesses all that you are doing and thinking, without judging or reacting to it. It stays clear, attentive and receptive.

△ The caring act of preparing food can be an ideal focus for meditation if, unlike this woman, you do not let distractions intrude. As you peel and slice, use all your senses to become fully aware of the food's texture, colour, scent and form.

"Wherever we go we have to take ourselves with us."
Traditional wisdom

written mantras

Likhit japa is the traditional practice of writing or drawing a mantra over and over again rather than chanting it aloud. The mantra that is most often used in this form of meditation is the symbol OM, which is carefully drawn repeatedly on a page while repeating the sound silently in your mind with each repetition of the symbol.

Like other repetitive tasks, likhit japa is a way to keep the mind focused and still. It is considered a powerful form of mantra use because it reinforces the habit of silent repetition of the mantra. It is a very pleasant and creative task to do in a meditation group – perhaps after lunch when everyone

The Story of the Sweeping Monk

There was once a Zen Buddhist monk who was given the task of maintaining the monastery garden. It was typical of such gardens – a simple courtyard spread with raked gravel, with a few large stones and potted plants arranged to create an atmosphere of peace and harmony. There was also a stately tree in the garden.

The monk swept up all the leaves that had fallen from the tree, deadheaded and tidied the plants, then raked the gravel in smooth sweeping strokes as he backed out toward the entrance. Just as he closed the gate a single leaf fell from the tree right into the middle of the courtyard. His fellow monks commiserated with him: "What a shame! Just when it was so perfect."

"Not at all," replied the gardener with a radiant smile, "I am simply being given another opportunity to serve." He opened the gate and walked across the gravel, disturbing its smoothness with his footprints. He picked up the leaf and calmly proceeded to back his way out again, raking the gravel as he went – still smiling, still focused, still enjoying his own company, still enveloped in deep peace and joy.

△ The story of the sweeping monk is an example of the spiritual enlightenment that can come from performing everyday tasks.

◁ When doing likhit japa, repeat the mantra silently in your head each time you draw the symbol, focusing your attention on its meaning. The aim is to preserve the rhythm of the repetitions, as if you were chanting the mantra.

▽ A written mantra such as the OM symbol can be used creatively, drawing with different coloured pencils to make a pattern or an original picture. Hindus sometimes write the symbols on birch bark or leaves, or use them to build up a picture of a deity.

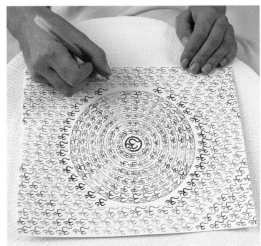

wants to relax – or at home alone as a way of unwinding.

The ways in which likhit japa can be performed seem infinite. Some Hindu monks keep a notebook and a pencil in their pocket and simply draw neat rows of OMs across the page whenever they have a spare moment. The aim is to fulfil a self-appointed task – such as drawing 100,000 OMs, perhaps aiming for a definite number on each page.

Other mantras can be copied out in a similar way, or you can use a Western phrase that is meaningful to you, such as "world peace", repeating it with intent that the world will become ever more peaceful as a result of your thought vibrations: every action starts with a thought, and if enough people think the same thought they can change the world. You can draw a symbol, such as a dove, to represent your repeated phrase, covering your page with a flock of birds that will continue to remind you of the thought that you sent out to bring

healing to the world while you were doing likhit japa meditation. There are many other familiar symbols that represent spiritual inspiration and which you could draw repeatedly in lines or patterns to reinforce the appropriate feelings in yourself – you might choose a rose to represent

△ Creating and contemplating a mandala, a symbolic representation of the universe, is another valuable form of meditation.

"unconditional love", a flame for "the divine presence within", or joined palms in prayer or greeting for "we are all one".

Hobbies and skills as meditation

Like exercise and rest, spending time on skills and crafts we love is an important element of a balanced, harmonious life that can lead us away from the negativity of tamas and the self-obsession of rajas. Learning new skills simply for the pleasure of doing so, and spending time on hobbies we enjoy, are ways in which we can relax and develop a sattvic attitude to life, which is the way to higher consciousness and the state of meditation.

a state of self-forgetfulness

Once you experience the fact that it is not so much what you do as how you do it that leads to a state of meditation in daily life, endless possibilities become available. This is the essence of *karma* yoga – actions performed in a state of self-forgetfulness. The sattvic state induces relaxed concentration on the task in hand simply because it is there to be done and enjoyed for its own sake.

Both tamas and rajas increase self-centredness, whereas sattva is an open state of unconditional welcome to each moment as it arises and to all the relationships contained therein. It is a state in which you can lose yourself in what you are doing – and find that you enjoy your own company as a result. This is why hobbies are so satisfying and an excellent way to develop sattvic qualities.

Creative writing, for example, can be a very meditative experience. You are alone with your thoughts and really have to get to know yourself. An excellent way to start is by writing a spiritual diary, containing your feelings, dreams and insights, which helps to develop self-awareness. If you enjoy painting, you can spend many happy hours observing and recording the beauties of nature. Or you can let your imagination run riot, as children do, and see what appears on the paper – this can also be very psychologically revealing and further develop your self-awareness.

△ Creative hobbies such as painting foster self-surrender: it is not how well you perform or the end result that matters, but your enjoyment of relating to your subject and materials.

▷ There is something intensely satisfying and releasing about the skill of making pots, where all your attention is concentrated on the symmetry of the shape you are creating and the feel of the clay.

◁ Focus on the creative and enjoyable aspects of your job – making work into a form of stimulating play – and you will increase its rewards. Approach mundane or difficult tasks with an attitude of self-discipline, to help you achieve what you set out to do to your own satisfaction.

▽ Supporting each other in interesting and rewarding pastimes brings a great deal of mutual pleasure, raises energy levels, and helps to create a harmonious, sattvic home.

making work into play

With practice, you can even turn the work you are paid to do into your favourite "hobby" if you approach it with the right attitude, so that you can honestly say "I am so lucky to be paid to do what I enjoy." Meditation practice can help you look for ways to get greater enjoyment from what you do for a living.

The reverse can also occur – an enjoyable hobby can become a tiresome burden if you feel under an obligation to deliver. The most interesting job or the most skilful

▷ Gardening brings the pleasure of watching plants grow and the feeling that you are working in harmony with nature.

pastime may become a chore if it is approached with a negative attitude. Patanjali's three "preliminary practices" – self-discipline, self-awareness and self-surrender – can help you restore your interest and pleasure.

Self-discipline is a contract you make with yourself to complete what you set out to do, regardless of whether any demands are being made on you by others. Self-awareness is the art of recognizing unwillingness and procrastination as an aspect of tamas and taking steps to renew your enthusiasm for the project (balancing with rajas) so that you can start again with an attitude of self-surrender and self-forgetfulness (sattva). Like the gunas, Patanjali's three qualities resemble the interwoven strands of a single rope and without all three of them, little of real worth or enjoyment can be accomplished.

Focusing the mind

◁ Modern life is made even more complex by technology that allows us to do several tasks at once. Concentrate on one thing at a time.

▷ When the phone rings, focus on it briefly rather than grabbing it immediately, giving yourself time to settle and prepare your mind.

Centripetal force is energy that flows from the edges to the middle, as when you pick up sensations from the surface of the body and register them consciously in the brain. All the practices that prepare for meditation have the quality of drawing energies back into your central self, into a deep pool or store. Using this energy, you can respond richly to life in a sattvic, conscious, focused and loving manner, directing your full attention to each task.

The demands of modern life can tempt you to attend to several things at once – with the result that nothing is done with full awareness, your attention is fragmented and you lose your sattvic outlook on life. Regular meditation practice helps you to recover a focused approach, dealing with each moment as it arises calmly and giving it your full attention.

pulling in opposite directions
According to the teachings of yoga the mind tends to function in two opposing ways: centrifugally and centripetally.

Centrifugal force is when energy is drawn away from the centre to the periphery, where it is dissipated and loses its force. This is what happens when you allow worldly attachments to grab and hold your attention, hang on to negative emotions and prejudices, or try to do everything at once. Spreading yourself too thinly without refocusing squanders your energies, letting them drain away like water being scattered across sand, so that you end up feeling depleted and unfulfilled. Wasting your vital forces in this way leads to stress, exhaustion and eventually to illness.

directed attention
"Alternating current" flowing between a subject (me) and an object (you) is a simple way to describe all relationships. This current needs to be focused rather than dissipated if relationships are to be nourishing and creative. The Sanskrit word for this is *ekagrata*. It means "one-pointedness" and refers to the process of gathering attention in from the periphery and then directing it on to a specific object. Ekagrata is a

▽ As you water a plant, focus on its beauty and the care you are giving it. Bringing the whole of your attention to each action is a form of meditation in itself, and makes any routine daily task more rewarding.

"TIME OUT" PREVENTS "BURNOUT"

Most of us need more time for ourselves and this can usually be achieved by following Patanjali's advice. Self-discipline enables you to say "no" and keep certain periods of the day sacrosanct for your own recharging and deep healing. With self-awareness, when you feel you are losing your focus you can stop to stretch, breathe, or repeat a mantra to bring you back into sattvic balance before proceeding. Self-surrender enables you to let go of all unnecessary or negative concerns, feelings or thoughts and to simplify your lifestyle, trusting in the divine guidance and support within yourself that is just waiting for you to draw upon it. Your "higher self" will never force its attentions upon you – it is up to you to seek within, to ask for help and to make time to be receptive to your inner voice through meditation.

△ When taking time out, find a private space and don't let yourself be distracted by other people, near and distant noises or worrying about other demands on your time. Cultivating self-awareness will give you the confidence to take a break when you need one.

rhythmical two-way mental process similar to the physical process of breathing in and out, and the emotional process of receiving sensations and responding appropriately. We are seldom fully aware of how much energy is tied up in long-term attachments, hopes, fears, plans and resentments that bind us to the past or future and prevent us from living fully in the present.

coping with life's demands

Modern technology often makes it possible to do several tasks at once. In the office you may be listening to instructions, designing a spreadsheet on a computer and taking a telephone call, but it is all too easy to forget part of the instructions, mess up the spreadsheet and be unhelpful to the caller. Domestic situations can dissipate energy in the same way – absentmindedly answering a child's questions while driving a car in heavy traffic having left late for an appointment, then forgetting to pick up the cleaning. The more you can release energy tied up in supporting negative emotions and thought patterns, the more will be available to support your busy life instead.

◁ Before going out to keep an appointment, a short meditation will help you to centre your energy and clear your mind.

Using the language of mudras

◁ The traditional postures for meditation are
designed to promote the flow of energy through
the koshas, but with regular practice the position
you adopt becomes a trigger that helps you gain
the meditative state. As you settle yourself into
your customary position (or mudra) your
breathing slows and deepens, mental chatter is
stilled and you can begin your journey inward.

also create a different mood within. When
you are feeling dull or irritable, pause to
breathe deeply and relax and see how your
mood improves.

the purpose of mudras

If you are in a sattvic mood you will radiate
relaxation and peacefulness simply by the
way you stand, move and sit. When you hold
your body in a sattvic pose, breathing
peacefully, alert yet relaxed, you actually
become sattvic – and this is the general
purpose of mudras. They alter the flow of
prana through the koshas and balance the
nervous systems. They use body language
to achieve specific results.

hand mudras

Hand positions (*hasta mudras*) reveal a great
deal. Many everyday positions demonstrate
a sattvic attitude: for example, a handshake
signifies trust and friendship (by offering
the hand in which you would traditionally
have held a weapon) and joining your palms
at your heart with a bow to accompany the
Indian greeting "Namaste" signifies respect
and love for another person.

Many energy circuits terminate at the
fingertips, as is well known in therapeutic
disciplines that "move" or "rebalance"
energies, such as acupuncture, shiatsu and
reflexology. By positioning the hands in
certain ways we can, therefore, reduce
negative feelings and enhance positive ones
by creating a positive flow of energy.

To begin with you may need to hold a
hand mudra for half an hour or so to feel
its subtle effects, but once you have practised

The Sanskrit word *mudra* means "attitude"or
"gesture". It refers to a physical position that
reflects our mood, changes our breathing
pattern or alters our state of consciousness.
The attitudes we strike, often unconsciously,
constitute our "body language", which other
people recognize and respond to. They
reveal how body and mind are a unity:
thought (mood) affects energy and energy
(movement) affects thought.

body language and the gunas

Someone in a tamasic mood will slouch and
droop, looking tired or bored or unco-
operative. A person in a rajasic mood will
show anger or excitement by thrusting the
chin forward aggressively, waving arms
about, or clenching fists. In each case a
change of posture can help to change the
mood. A different stance not only conveys
a different message to other people, but can

△ Once you are practised in using hand mudras, try creating meditative sequences from a range of different positions, or invent mudras of your own. You could devise a graceful "hand dance" that promotes a serene, contemplative state.

and become thoroughly familiar with it, adopting it will immediately produce the desired sattvic effect.

You can use a hand mudra unobtrusively, as an instant trigger that changes your energies. An example is the use of a mala (or Christian rosary or Muslim worry beads). If you practise regularly it is enough, in difficult situations, to simply visualize yourself passing your mala beads through your hand (using your inner senses of sight and touch) to evoke a sattvic mood and feel centred and at peace.

HAND MUDRAS

There are a great many hand mudras that can help you to remain in a peaceful sattvic state in any situation.

◁ *Gyana mudra*: This mudra is used for practising meditation. The tip of the thumb (cosmic consciousness) is joined to the tip of the index finger (individual or personality consciousness), so that the energies are harmonized. Often the fingernail of the index finger is pressed into the cleft between the root of the thumb and the rest of the hand to represent letting go of the ego in surrender to the greater good. This mudra can help you to restrain your self-centred impulses whenever you feel threatened.

◁ *Yoni mudra*: Join your palms, then clasp the middle (sattva), ring (rajas) and little (tamas) fingers together, so that the energies mingle. Open the palms, keeping the index finger and thumb tips joined, with the index fingers (ego) pointing down and thumbs (cosmic consciousness) pointing up. This mudra protects you by taking your energies inward and back to the source (*yoni* means "womb"). Use it in crowded places, when you are travelling or wherever there are angry or disturbed energies.

◁ *Bhairava mudra* (for men), *bhairavi mudra* (for women): The Buddha is often portrayed using this mudra. Men place the right palm over the left, and women the left over the right, both palms facing up with fingers relaxed. The thumb tips may touch to close the energy circuits. This mudra focuses your energy for meditation or to maintain inner peace when relating to others. The *anjali mudra* is similar, but with the hands more open in a gesture of prayerful pleading.

◁ *Shankha mudra* (the conch shell): Fold the fingers of your right hand around your left thumb, covering the back of the right hand with your left fingers. Touch your right thumb tip to your left index fingertip and place your hands in your lap. A conch shell, when placed to your ear, makes a sound like the sea – it is one of the sounds of *nada*, the inner vibration. When you blow into a conch shell it sounds like OM, the primordial vibration, recalling the vibrational basis of all phenomena.

◁ *Sakat mudra*: This mudra is used to control anger. Spread the palms and point the index (ego) finger of each hand downward to release pent-up tension that might otherwise escape in angry words. Press the thumb tips (cosmic consciousness) together to unblock the preoccupation with what is unimportant in the greater scheme of things.

Sample
Meditations

The meditations in this chapter are designed
to help you to a deeper understanding of
your own evolutionary path into the wisdom
and love of your soul nature. The previous
chapters have shown why it is so important
to become balanced at all levels and why the
traditional "good" qualities are the natural
expression of our higher selves. Practising the
meditations described on the following pages
can bring healing to your relationships and
even to the planet.

Meditating on: the five yamas

Patanjali, the great master of classical yoga, based his system of eight limbs on the ethical foundation of the yamas. These five precepts deal with personal integrity, self-restraint and respect for other people and all forms of life, and Patanjali presents them as "abstentions" to be practised in thought, word and deed. If we could return instantly to a state of sattva every time rajas or tamas became inappropriate we would automatically be practising Patanjali's yamas, known collectively as "the great vow" or "rules for living".

By making one of the yamas the focus of a contemplative meditation, we can explore the ideas it presents and gain insights that we can continue to reflect and act on after the meditation, thus improving our interactions with the wider world and with other people.

ahimsa

Together we form "society", yet exploitation of the weak and vulnerable, causing infinite pain and distress, underlies the competitive structure of our modern materialist society and is responsible for much of the misery in the world. *Ahimsa* is abstention from violence, aggression, domination and harm to any living thing, including human beings, and this first precept, which is central to the concept of "right living", is common to all the world's great religions and underpins the other four yamas.

△ **The essence of the five yamas is that they promote an attitude of acceptance, respect and love for people around you as they are, rather than as commodities for exploitation.**

satya

The principle of *satya* is abstention from falsehood, deceit, concealment and economy with the truth. Global advertising, big

DISCURSIVE OR CONTEMPLATIVE MEDITATION

The meditation on the yamas featured on these pages is a contemplative, or discursive, kind of meditation. With this type of meditation awareness is focused upon a concept – rather than a sensation or a physical object – to bring new understanding. The thoughts that arise concerning the chosen idea are observed without judgment and can be written down as they occur to you without disturbing either the focus or the train of thought. Have paper and pen beside you before you start the meditation so that you can record your insights immediately or soon after meditating, before they have faded from your mind. You will be surprised at the depth and clarity of your new ideas: they may change your whole attitude to concepts or feelings that you were previously unaware of, or took for granted.

contemplative meditation

Allow at least half an hour of uninterrupted time for contemplative meditation on one of Patanjali's yamas. Later you may wish to spend longer. A timer can be useful, so that you know when to start coming out of your meditation, leaving enough time to ground yourself and write down the insights you have gained in order to reflect upon them later.

△ **1** Sit with your spine erect and stretch and settle your body into a relaxed, alert position by stretching the arms overhead, with the fingers intertwined.

△ **2** Lowering your elbows to shoulder level, concentrate your attention on your breathing, lifting and opening the chest.

△ **3** Open your hands and let them rest, palms up, on your knees. You may like to repeat a mantra for a few moments, or the name of the yama you plan to explore, to settle yourself into a sattvic state.

business, politicians and the media break this abstention at every turn. The desire to hoodwink others – purposely eroding the boundaries between truth and falsehood – arises from a lack of respect for them. Patanjali's practice of self-awareness, which helps us to see and accept ourselves as we are, allows us to see more clearly through self-deception and intentional distortion wherever they occur, to be less seduced by glamour and hype and more focused on values that are genuine.

asteya

Self-interest and the profit motive stem from the belief that "what is yours is mine and what is mine is also mine". *Asteya* is abstention from theft, taking advantage,

giving less than is due, getting something for nothing and all other forms of exploitation. Patanjali's practice of self-surrender loosens the grip of "me and mine" until we realize that we own nothing: we enter the world at birth without possessions and leave them behind when we die. Everything that we use and enjoy in life is only on loan.

brahmacharya

This is abstention from lust and greed, which are disrespectful and rajasic and cause us to dissipate our life energies. Modern society is increasingly obsessed with sexual gratification, and we are encouraged by liberalism and advertising to feel entitled to take whatever we desire. *Brahmacharya* is

associated with sexual abstinence, but actually concerns lust and greed of all kinds. It is about respecting the life force within ourselves and directing it toward personal evolution rather than personal gratification. Loving partnership supports life and evolution, whereas lust does not.

aparigraha

The fifth yama is abstention from acquiring and hoarding possessions for their own sake, seeing ourselves in terms of what we have rather than who we are. Keeping life simple prevents us from tying up time, money and energy worrying about mere things. It frees us to focus on more rewarding pursuits and relationships and upon living fully rather than on the pursuit of lifeless things.

Meditating on: opposing qualities

◁ The ultimate aim of meditation is the transcendent state of samadhi, in which the truth is clearly seen. It has been likened by the scholar I.K. Taimni to the experience of a pilot flying out of a cloud bank into bright sunlight.

through sharing. Bad feelings in the light chakras result from confusion and a sense of disconnectedness, whereas good feelings come with understanding and access to higher wisdom.

Transcendence depends upon cultivating and maintaining good feelings and a positive outlook on life. Gratitude, acceptance, respect and personal responsibility are just some of the positive qualities of the yamas. Positive qualities make us feel good – even to reflect on them brings peace and joy, helping to lead us inward toward a state of deep meditation, which we can experience in the balanced, contented sattvic state. Having entered the meditation in a sattvic state the chosen object of meditation can further deepen our good feelings.

meditating on opposites

Taking one obstacle that is currently hindering you as the focus of a contemplative meditation can be very helpful, provided you can accept that it is just "one face of the coin" – the negative face – and aim to bring it into balance so that it no longer disturbs you. Ask yourself what is its opposite face – the positive and sattvic aspect? Having established that, and having truly felt the positive as keenly as you previously felt the negative, you are ready for the most important question: what is the "substance" of the coin that is now showing you its two complementary faces?

Opposites are always complementary parts of a greater whole, the poles that connect the energy of a continuum – nothing either good or bad exists in isolation. This type of meditation brings a much wider perspective on life and frees you from the "slavery of the opposites".

Meditation increases self-awareness, but this alone is not enough to achieve lasting change and spiritual evolution. If we are to transcend the programming created and reinforced by our genes and conditioning, we also need to engage self-discipline and self-surrender. All the different kinds of energy in the chakras need to be balanced and working together.

good and bad feelings

We feel bad in the life chakras if we are hungry (feeling lack), embarrassed (feeling fear of criticism) or angry (feeling thwarted) and we experience good feelings when eating a delicious meal, socializing happily or moving toward a goal. Bad feelings in the love chakras arise from self-centredness and blocked self-expression, and good feelings

PAIRS OF OPPOSITES

Patanjali described the yamas in terms of abstention from certain forms of behaviour that are all at the negative end of a spectrum. In order to follow his precepts, we need to understand the positive forms of behaviour that are their opposites, at the other end of the spectrum:

- **Ahimsa** is abstention from **violence** – harming or hurting any living being.
  The opposite of violence is gratitude, acceptance, respect and personal responsibility for looking after all forms of life.

- **Satya** is abstention from **falsehood** – distortion of the truth as we understand it.
  The opposite of falsehood is gratitude, acceptance, respect and personal responsibility for expressing the truth as clearly as we can.

- **Asteya** is abstention from **theft** – taking what we are not entitled to.
  The opposite of theft is gratitude, acceptance, respect and personal responsibility for managing with the resources allocated to us.

- **Brahmacharya** is abstention from **incontinence** – squandering life energies through lust.
  The opposite of incontinence is gratitude, acceptance, respect and personal responsibility for the forces of life within us and the enjoyment of our senses.

- **Aparigraha** is abstention from **acquisitiveness** – coveting and hoarding material things.
  The opposite of acquisitiveness is gratitude, acceptance, respect and personal responsibility for the processes of life-light-love.

coin meditation

This meditation starts with experiencing opposites and then discovering the quality that encompasses them both – the substance of the coin itself. Simple examples include hot/cold, the two faces of temperature; rough/smooth, the two faces of texture; love/hate, the two faces of a relationship. The deeper the qualities of the opposites the more likely it is that their substance proves to be love.

▷ **1** Prepare yourself for meditation so that you are in a sattvic state.

△ **2** Imagine that you have a bag containing coins. Each unknown coin has two faces, one representing a negative quality and the other its positive opposite.

△ **3** Take out a coin and stroke one side of it, allowing any feeling – one of a pair of opposites – to develop. Whatever arises, stay with it. Then experience its opposite quality equally intensely, before discovering the quality that encompasses both "faces" of the coin. Come out of meditation slowly. After the meditation make sure that you stretch and ground yourself thoroughly.

△ Negative feelings stand in the way of self-awareness and self-expression, and can isolate us from one another. A meditation on opposites can help to remove emotional obstacles by helping us to understand how all such feelings are only a part of a larger whole.

Meditating on: the path to freedom

◁ The meditative journey of spiritual evolution leads us away from the darkness of fear toward the light of unclouded truth.

The transcendent state of total liberation of mind and body is known by different names in different religious traditions – *samadhi*, the state of unclouded truth, union with the divine, and so on – but the meaning is always the same. It is a serene state in which the ultimate truth of existence is revealed and the soul becomes one with universal, unchanging consciousness. We can step on to the path that leads to this spiritual freedom when we decide to change ourselves, whatever our circumstances – rather than blaming the rest of the world for our problems.

overcoming obstacles and distractions

Patanjali teaches that the practice of meditation is the "royal path" to samadhi because it weakens the obstacles that lie in the way of change and spiritual growth: illness, fatigue, doubt, carelessness, laziness, attachment, delusion, failure to achieve and failure to maintain progress.

All these familiar obstacles are manifestations of tamas and rajas. We know from our own experience that they can all agitate the mind, weaken the body and obstruct the spirit, distracting us from following the true path.

focusing on uplifting states

Once we have erased our negative states through meditation, we need to move on to contemplation of those uplifting states that Patanjali assures us precede the ultimate state of samadhi:

- **Trust** (an aspect of self-surrender). Spiritual masters tell us that only two emotions – fear and love – really exist, and that of these two fear is an illusion that we can simply drop when we are ready to do so. Letting go of fear is the great surrender, and enables us to surrender all the other needs that hold us back, such as:
  - **staying in control**, together with all the rajasic effort this involves
  - **protecting ourselves**, instead of co-operating cheerfully with life's natural processes
  - **promoting ourselves** – and attaching too much importance to success in the eyes of the world
  - **needing to justify our existence**, when our existence is really justification in itself
  - **holding on to limiting perceptions of who we are**, instead of revelling in being essential to the glory and wholeness of life, light and love.

- **Perseverance** (an aspect of self-discipline), with regular practice and a daily routine enables us to maintain our enthusiasm and determination.
- **Recollection** (an aspect of self-awareness) reinforces what we have learned, as we test our new skills and insights at every opportunity in daily life. Driving instructors often tell their pupils that they only really start learning to drive after passing their test and the same is true for meditators. Every "test" becomes an opportunity.
- **Tranquillity** (the state of sattva) becomes second nature once we can combine self-discipline with self-awareness and self-surrender.
- **Wisdom** (through meditation) brings us to the end of our spiritual path – for in the state of boundless freedom there are no paths at all.

△ Others can tell us how they have discovered their own truth through meditation, but we have to realize for ourselves that we can choose to let go of fear and embrace freedom.

> "Do not believe anything because you have heard it – even from the wise – or read it in any book. Believe it only if it accords with your own experience."
>
> *Buddha*

the seagull: soaring toward freedom

These movements will help you to free yourself from distractions and focus upon the heart chakra, where you embrace uplifting states, accept and balance emotions, heal past traumas, forgive others and yourself and let go of all hurt, anger and resentment. The seagull lives totally in the present moment, as it soars through the skies. Visualize yourself flying high in the blue sky and let all negativity go, releasing it as you breathe out and filling the space in your heart with fresh glory on each breath in.

▷ **1** Sit on your heels in Virasana and bring your palms together at the heart chakra in namaste mudra.

△ **2** As you breathe out, bend forward and place your forehead on the floor, keeping your hands and elbows as high as possible and stretching your chest. Surrender and empty your lungs.

△ **3** As you breathe in, sit up, lift your sternum and stretch your arms like wings wide to the sides. Look up and joyfully surrender to the air, the moment and the movement. Surrender and fill your lungs. Repeat for several minutes.

Meditating on: the OM mantra

Patanjali begins his list of meditations with: "Complete surrender to the almighty Lord...who is expressed through the sound of the sacred syllable OM. It should be repeated and its essence realized." (From A. Shearer's translation of the *Sutras*.) OM, or Aum, is recognized in many cultures as the primordial sound, whose vibration brought the universe into being. Repetition of the OM mantra on a daily basis, chanted aloud, whispered or repeated silently, has a cumulative and profoundly beneficial effect.

When chanted aloud (intoned rather than sung), the OM sound – pronounced as in "home" – should be deep and full, with the vibrations resonating in the life chakras, then moving up into the chest and the love chakras, and finally closing with a long,

humming "mmm" in the head and the light chakras – all on one deep steady note. Overtones may sometimes be heard. These are the faint sounds of the same note at higher octaves, as when groups of Buddhist monks chant in a deep resonant rumble, with the overtones wafting above like celestial choirs.

a–u–m

The syllable can also be divided into three sounds – A (the created beginning), U (the sustained now) and M (the dissolution of creation). This trinity corresponds to sat-chit-ananda. A is the beginning of life, time and forms; U is maintained through the relationships of cosmic love; M comes when we experience personally that all is spirit – and the rest is mental illusion.

△ **The Sanskrit symbol of the sacred syllable OM is often used as an object on which to focus. Place it on a low table so that you can concentrate your gaze on it during your meditation practice.**

chanting with a mala

The mala has 108 beads. It should always be held in the right hand and passed between thumb (representing universal consciousness) and middle finger (representing sattva guna). One bead is passed with each repetition of the mantra. Start from the larger bead (*sumeru*) and, when you come round to it again, do not cross it but turn the mala and go back for another round.

1 Sit in a meditation pose and settle your body and breathing.

◁ **2** Hold the mala in a comfortable position (traditional positions are near your heart or on your right knee).

3 As you breathe in chant OM silently. As you breathe out chant OM aloud (or silently), then move to the next bead on the mala and repeat 107 times. If your mind wanders bring it back gently to the mantra.

4 Sit for a few moments and feel the vibrations of the sound within you, before grounding yourself. The sensation of these vibrations creates a trigger for you – recalling them at other times will take you back instantly to the sattvic state you were in while chanting.

"This Self, beyond all words, is the syllable OM.
This syllable, though indivisible, consists of three letters – A–U–M
[representing three states of being]...The fourth [state], the Self,
is OM...the supreme good, the One without a second. Whosoever
knows OM, the self, becomes the Self."

Mandukya Upanishad

chanting the mantra in a group meditation

This meditation is particularly effective when done in a group. Each person sounds his or her own note, all taking a breath in together (as indicated by the leader) and then chanting A, U, or M on the slow breath out. The meditation ends with everyone chanting OM on their own note and in their own rhythm, so that the sounds mingle together until a natural pause occurs. Silence follows until the meditation ends with a grounding ritual. The more people who join in the OM chanting the more powerful the effects become and the longer the subsequent silence is likely to continue.

△ **1** Sit in a circle in a comfortable meditation pose with spine erect and sternum lifted. Place the hands in front of the body with palms facing the lower abdomen and fingertips just touching. Breathe in together and chant A (aah...) on a deep note on the breath out, to resonate in the life chakras in the abdomen. Repeat this sound at least twice more, to energize and remove blockages.

△ **2** Move the hands up, with palms in front of the heart and fingertips just touching. Breathe in together and chant U (oooh...) on the breath out to resonate in the love chakras. Notice the different quality of the sound and the vibrations. Repeat twice more, feeling your own sound resonating within you.

△ **3** Move the hands overhead, stretching up and out in a joyful expression of complete freedom, palms facing forward. Look up (without compressing the neck) and breathe in together. Breathe out to chant M (mmm...) into the skull cavity and the light chakras, experiencing the sound within. Repeat twice more, then bring your hands down and remain silent. Finally chant OM, each in your own rhythm and pitch, until the group naturally falls silent. Sit in this silence for a while.

△ **4** Finish by bringing hands and forehead to the floor in a gesture of grounding and complete surrender.

DHARMA AND KARMA
OM is said to be the sound of creation, harmony and order. The eternal being expressed through the sound of OM is not the personal deity of any religion but the super-conscious organizing principle that sustains the divine order (*dharma*) by means of cause and effect (*karma*), and whose wisdom is available to all human beings as "the teacher of even the most ancient tradition of teachers".

▷ **OM is the sound vibration that underlies every part of the universe, down to the smallest detail.**

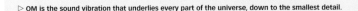

Meditating on: the chakras

◁ **Most of us have a dominant type of chakra energy, and traditional correspondences can help to define the basic character of the chakras. Each of the four lower chakras corresponds to one of the four elements.**

The chakras, which exist at the energy level, can be thought of as transformers that process the energy from all the koshas through our bodyminds into the physical world. The body, mind and emotions are all extensions of chakra function. Changes at one level will bring automatic changes at every other level.

The chakras are vortices of energy within our own being that we can become aware of for ourselves and then work with to balance and activate all levels of our being. We can gain a wealth of psychological insight by using meditation to explore the qualities traditionally attributed to each of the major chakras.

awareness of the chakras

To gain true insight into yourself, you need to understand the current state of your own chakra system – and this means becoming aware of it. To help you do this, work through the series of three meditative breathing routines that follows. You should bring focused awareness and discrimination to your exploration, so that, whatever your meditation may reveal, you can remain an impartial observer and learn from the experience, rather than getting carried away by it – especially if emotional responses catch you unawares.

As you explore your chakras during the meditation, try to feel each one's individual brightness or dullness. All the chakras spin, giving off light, colour, sensation and sound, and it is by picking up these subjective phenomena that you can assess if or when a particular chakra is under- or overactive within the system as a whole.

"Balance comes when we can accept and get along with everyone without compromising what we believe in. The balancing of the chakras and the flowering of each one brings us to Patanjali's "state of unclouded truth" and heaven on earth."

Author

CHAKRA CORRESPONDENCES

Each of us has a mix of influences, but one particular influence is usually dominant. Like each sign of the astrological zodiac, each chakra is associated with an element, which can help us to recognize its basic character. The four lower chakras display the following characters:

Capricorn   Taurus   Virgo

Pisces   Cancer   Scorpio

Aries   Leo   Sagittarius

Aquarius   Gemini   Libra

1 The base chakra (muladhara) corresponds with the element of Earth – as do the star signs of Capricorn, Taurus and Virgo. Their characteristics ensure survival, and among them are practicality, reliability, tenacity, logic, and a generally materialistic and no-nonsense approach to life. An Earth weakness can be a rigid and unimaginative outlook, unless it is tempered by other influences. If Earth is blocked we fail to ensure that we have the wherewithal to survive and if it is overactive we are obsessed with protecting ourselves by acquiring possessions.

2 The sacral chakra (svadisthana) corresponds to the element of Water – as do the signs of Pisces, Cancer, and Scorpio, whose characteristics ensure social bonding. Among them are empathy, enjoyment, sensuality, homemaking and caring for others. A Water weakness can be a tendency to tearfulness, emotional sensitivity and slipping into overindulgence to avoid facing facts. If Water is blocked we may become outcasts from society, upon whose acceptance our lives depend, and if it is overactive we may become addicted to substances, pleasures or people.

3 The navel chakra (manipura) corresponds to the element of Fire – as do the signs of Aries, Leo and Sagittarius, whose characteristics enable us to achieve personal success. They include warmth and friendliness, enthusiasm and zeal to inspire others to believe in themselves and their opinions. A Fire weakness is the tendency to burn out through overconfidence and ignoring obstacles. If Fire is blocked we lack the energy to plan or achieve anything and drift helplessly through life, and if it is overactive we develop inflated egos.

4 The heart chakra (anahata) corresponds to the element of Air – as do the signs of Aquarius, Gemini and Libra. Their main characteristic is to reach beyond the ego to other people, beauty and harmony, ideas and ideals. Air is a property shared by all, and Air signs understand that we are all interactive parts of a greater whole. An Air weakness is a tendency to be disorganized and unrealistic, though well-meaning. If Air is blocked we are imprisoned by our ego and if it is overactive we do not recognize boundaries.

Chakras 1–3 are the life chakras that combine to maintain physical life for the individual. Chakras 1–4 can be perceived as forming the base that supports the three "higher" elements: Ether (or communication), Mind (the organ of consciousness) and Spirit (the link with the whole).

1 chakra awareness: "switching on the light"

First, settle yourself into a suitable position for meditation practice to promote a sattvic state. Awareness is a function of the brow (ajna) chakra, so this meditation begins by "switching on the light".

▷ A good "switching on" practice is tratak – focused gazing for a few moments upon an object such as a candle flame, flower or crystal. This balances the nervous system and focuses energy in the centre of the head to light up the mind. Alternatively, you could perform a short breathing practice, such as alternate nostril breathing.

continued over page ▷

2 chakra awareness: breathing up and down the spine

This sequence will make you sensitive to the energy pathway upon which the chakras are located, like roundabouts or junctions on the busy highway that lies within the spinal cord.

1 First breathe in and "drive" up the motorway from the tailbone to the top of the head.

▷ **2** Breathe out and drive back down again. Alternatively, you can imagine drawing light up on the breath in and letting it release back down on the breath out – like mercury rising and falling in a thermometer. You may like to feel the flow of breath with your hands as you practise this exercise.

3 chakra awareness: stopping at each chakra

You should really feel the quality of each major chakra as you practise the following meditation.

1 At the base of the spine breathe in and out of the base chakra. Energy is concentrated at this point on the breath in and radiates outward as it is released on the breath out. Repeat twice more before moving up to the next chakra point, the sacral. Again, breathe in to focus energy in the chakra and breathe out to allow it to radiate outward.

2 Continue up the spine with three breaths to activate each chakra point. After breathing into the crown chakra three times, pause and rest, letting its energies inspire and heal you, then start the downward journey, beginning with the crown chakra. After reaching and breathing in and out of the base chakra three times, pause and rest again – feeling the nurturing support and safe solidity of the physical plane upon which you live. The aim is to restore balance between the chakras by understanding and putting right what is causing imbalances.

3 Repeat the whole process once or twice more in a slow, relaxed and observant manner. Then come out of your meditation gently and ground yourself throroughly.

◁ **4** Once out of the meditation, you may like to record your experience to help you reinforce your increasing sensitivity to the different "feel" of each chakra.

chanting the chakra bija mantras

Once you have located your chakras and can breathe in and out of them easily, you may like to explore chanting to brighten them up or nourish them. Each chakra has its own sound (see box below). These are *bija*, or "seed" mantras, which have no literal meaning but are designed to plant the seed of a concept in the mind. They should each be chanted three times on a low, slow note that vibrates in tune with the chakra's own vibratory rate. The Sanskrit sound "AM" is soft – somewhere between "ham", "hum" and "harm".

▷ **1** Start at the base chakra and chant in each chakra all the way up. Pause after chanting in the crown chakra, then start again at the crown chakra and move down, pausing again after chanting into the base chakra.

2 Repeat the whole cycle twice more before coming out of the meditation. The bija mantras are represented by Sanskrit letters placed within a symbol that you may also like to visualize.

THE SOUNDS OF THE CHAKRAS

As you chant these sounds, think of the qualities of each chakra, expressed perfectly by their particular symbol.

- **LAM** for the **base chakra (muladhara)**, placed within a **yellow square** (the compact quality of earth).

- **VAM** for the **sacral chakra (svadisthana)**, placed within a **white crescent moon** (the moon governs the waters).

- **RAM** for the **navel chakra (manipura)**, placed within a **red triangle pointing downward** (fire spreads upward and outward from a single point).

- **YAM** for the **heart chakra (anahata)**, placed at the centre of **two interlaced triangles** (the colour varies, as does the colour of air, which joins heaven and earth together).

- **HAM** for the **throat chakra (vishuddhi)**, placed within a **white circle** (ether or space pervades the entire universe).

- **AUM** for the **brow chakra (ajna)**, placed within a **grey or mauve circle between two petals**. This is the "command centre" where all opposites (the two petals) merge and are transcended through awareness and understanding.

- **OM** for the **crown chakra (sahasrara)**, placed at the **centre of a sphere of light** radiating in all directions – spirit pervades all creation.

Meditating on: vibrating with the universe

Inside every atom is another medium that no one can perceive, however well equipped with the latest technology. The molecules in solids, liquids and gases are all made up of atoms that consist almost entirely of empty space. It has been claimed that the "solid matter" in any atom is no larger than a bee buzzing in the dome of some huge cathedral – the rest is space. The water lily that is the subject of the meditation described on the opposite page is an illusion, however beautiful and inspiring it may look. So are our thoughts about it. It is an illusion that the world is made up of solid, liquid or gaseous "things" because "no-thingness" is actually the reality.

creating space in our lives
Coming to terms with this concept of the physical world can change our perception of our own existence. Meditation helps us to see our opinions, thoughts and beliefs about the world as if they are in a film projected by our minds on to a screen. If we can learn to watch this picture show like an impartial observer, our personal dramas – which can seem so overwhelming when we are immersed in them – become more transparent and less consuming.

We begin to notice spaces between our thoughts, and pause before we automatically react to situations. There is more space in our life for relating wholeheartedly to other people. Once we can relax and enjoy the presence of this space in our lives it becomes our constant companion and friend, the divine all within every "thing".

connecting with the universe
We are the sum total not only of what we have been, but also of what we are now and what we may become. Our evolutionary journey is recorded in our genes and also (according to Hindu and Buddhist thought) in the mystical "akashic records" where our karma is balanced over many lifetimes in

△ **Meditating on the infinite space around us, and the infinite space within us, we are able to feel the harmony of the universe.**

various stages of being. Meditation can help us access this primary storehouse of knowledge, and to feel part of the vast system of the universe, rather than an isolated fragment.

hearing nada
Our universe began with a sound – OM, the primordial syllable – and every atom vibrates at its own frequency. We can further tune into our place in the system by learning to recognize our own internal sounds, or nada. Each of us can become aware of our own personal vibratory note when we insulate the senses from distraction during meditation and turn all our attention inward. Focus on nada calms the mind and brings greater spiritual and physical awareness to our lives.

chanting through the chakras

This powerful practice, which involves chanting a musical scale through the chakras, can help you to perceive and recognize nada, the inner vibration or sounds.

▷ **1** You can chant OM in each chakra, drumming to accompany the chanting if you wish. Start with any comfortably low note and ascend a scale to finish an octave higher. In the West, the key of C is often used, chanting C for the base chakra, D for the sacral chakra and so on. After A for the brow chakra you need another chakra on which to chant B, so focus upon *bindu* (the point at the back of the head where Buddhist monks sometimes wear a tuft of hair). The crown chakra then becomes C, an octave above the base chakra. This octave represents the "human" realm.

2 The octave above the crown chakra represents the "divine" realm and the one below the base chakra is the "animal" (or subhuman) realm. We have chakras in all three realms and many more – each of these will resonate as you chant.

3 Ascend and descend through the chakras three times before pausing in silence to feel the effects, then ground yourself thoroughly.

Meditation on a Water Lily

Meditating on the growth of a water lily will help you to understand the concept of the "great chain of being", and to find your own vibratory note within it. The chain concept forms the basis of the mystical Kabbala in the West and the chakra system in the East. Human beings are the link between the vibrationally lower and higher states of being – none being better or worse than another. The evolutionary path naturally leads up to greater complexity and higher consciousness, but however high we rise we remain firmly attached to the point where we began: rather than moving, we have expanded our entire being.

The growth of the lotus or water lily illustrates the spanning of different "realms" or states. Some ideas for a meditation on this subject are suggested here, but your own intuition can add many other insights:

- **The solid state (life):** The plant begins at the bottom of the lake, with a tiny root delving into the solid mud from where it draws its nourishment for life. The mud is heavy, sticky, messy, smelly and uncompromising – yet it is full of nutrients that are essential to the lily plant's survival. It also provides a firm foundation and anchors the plant by its roots, corresponding to our own animal, physical state that anchors us in our current incarnation.
- **The liquid state (light):** The tiny plant grows a stem that slowly rises up through the water, instinctively drawn towards the shimmering light. Water represents the flow of our emotions and thoughts. Just as its permeability to light helps tiny shoots to explore and grow into leaves and buds, so the

experiences that we encounter during our lives teach us our lessons, helping us to expand our sensitivity and awareness.
- **The gaseous state (love):** Eventually the leaves and buds of the water lily reach the surface and are exposed to the warmth of the air above the water. Here the flower opens under the touch of the sun and blissfully surrenders its beauty and perfume. It is fertilized with pollen from another flower so that, as the flower dies, the new seeds grow and drop into the mud at the bottom of the lake to start the cycle once more. Surrender is the essence of love and new life.

▽ **The lily grows up into the air, yet remains rooted in the earth.**

Meditating on: hearts and minds

"Placing the mind in the heart" is a famous Buddhist concept, shared by every spiritual tradition. The mind is a marvellous tool – processing sensual information and directing the body to act accordingly, observing, reflecting, learning from our past experiences, judging and making decisions, planning for the future. It is the activities of the heart, however, that make the world go round, as love is expressed as relating, interacting, sharing, giving and receiving.

the divine spark

The energy of the heart lies at the core of our existence, and our heartfelt attitudes drive our lives. In modern society the mind, with its ability to create technical marvels, is afforded our ultimate respect and the qualities of the heart are downgraded – yet the mind is always subservient to the heart and we "follow our heart" even when it leads us in a direction contrary to our better judgment. The teachings of every spiritual tradition insist that our minds (light) and our ego personalities (life) exist to serve the divine spark in us all that resides within our hearts (love).

▷ **The eternal flame – the divine spark within the heart of every being – is the subject of the meditation on the cave of the heart.**

"The ancient effulgent being, the indwelling Spirit, subtle, deep-hidden in the lotus [chakra] of the heart, is hard to know... Smaller than the smallest, greater than the greatest, this Self forever dwells within the hearts of all. One who is free from desire, with mind and senses purified, beholds the glory of the Self and is without sorrow."

Katha Upanishad

meditation on the "cave of the heart"

Our "heart home" is a sacred haven, untouched by any negativity, where we can feel safe, supported and healed. This meditation will help you to find this home.

1 Get settled into a still and peaceful state and prepare to visualize.

2 Imagine seeing yourself from a distance, sitting in your meditation pose within a luminous bubble that is suspended in space between heaven and earth. The sphere is your aura. A silvery cord attaches it firmly to heaven, then passes through your body seated in the centre of your aura and attaches it firmly to the earth.

3 Now look within your aura. The silver cord that passes through your body has your chakras strung along it like beads on a necklace.

4 Imagine yourself breathing deeply, seated inside your aura. As you breathe in you are, at the same time, drawing light down from the heavenly end of the cord and life up from the earthly end of the cord. As you breathe out, you puff this mixture into your aura, as though into a balloon, so that it gets brighter and bigger. Continue pumping both light (consciousness) and life (vitality) into your aura until it feels radiant and healthy.

5 See yourself sitting in your "mind space" in your skull, which is like a room with a front wall of mirrored glass. You can look through it to see the external world, but it also reflects back to you your own thoughts and mental pictures.

6 Imagine yourself standing up to leave your "mind space" and going down, either by a lift or a staircase, to the level of your "heart space".

7 On this level is a door. Open it reverently and walk into the "cave of your heart", where you see a low table, upon which a small lamp is burning – the eternal divine flame, the symbol of who you really are. This is who we all are, at heart.

8 Around the table are low benches. Sit down and gaze into the flame, letting its warmth and joy permeate and heal you at every level. Feel connected to your divine self.

9 When you are ready, let the scene dissolve and give it to the earth by breathing out deeply. Let it all go – a gift of peace and joy from you to our beleaguered planet.

10 Come out of meditation slowly, grounding yourself and perhaps writing down your experience. Repeat this meditation until it becomes so familiar that you can "take your mind into your heart" whenever you wish, and rest in the healing presence that abides there.

△ **Visualize your essential, eternal self as a lamp burning steadily in the cave of your heart.**

UNCONDITIONAL LOVE

Ananda maya kosha – the soul body – is the kosha of our highest wisdom. It contains our past experience and knows our future purpose. Unlike the mind, it experiences only unconditional love, however negative we may be feeling at our mental and emotional levels. It can be very helpful to invite into your heart the soul of a person who is causing you difficulties at the personality level. Since all souls love each other, deep healing can occur when two souls meet in the divine presence of the eternal flame, even though the other person is unaware of this meeting at a conscious level.

▷ **The practice of meditation allows us to gain access to our highest levels of consciousness, where our souls meet in loving kindness.**

Meditating on: living life at soul level

It is through meditation that we truly experience our "soul level". We learn to listen to our own souls, and to reach out to other souls and the world around us – as in the group meditation on these pages.

the inner teacher

When we feel in need of help or guidance in our journey to the soul, we can call upon a source of higher wisdom. This can be our higher self, or a great master such as the Buddha, or any appropriate figure from our belief system. Whoever we invite may enter the privacy of our heart and answer our questions. By learning to ask, listen to this guidance and trust our innermost promptings, we can channel this higher wisdom into our lives.

▷ **A group meditation is a powerful expression of universal oneness, uniting all the members in loving co-operation. It is usually directed at a specific goal, such as healing.**

healing group meditation

This meditation directs group energy to heal a specific person, the whole group or the whole planet. It can last 10–20 minutes and be led silently by one person sitting in the group, who rings a small bell to start each section, so that everyone proceeds as one.

1 Sit in a circle facing a candle in the centre – this represents the person or group in need of healing, or the whole planet and all living beings. Allow the group time to get settled.

2 Light the candle to begin the meditation.

3 Section 1: Each person connects with above (light) and below (life) and, on each breath in, draws light down and life up simultaneously into the group aura, like a huge balloon that encompasses the whole group and the flame at its centre.

4 On each breath out this group aura becomes filled with love energy, and grows ever brighter. Continue this section of the meditation for a few minutes, strengthening the group aura.

5 Section 2: Breathe light and life in as before and breathe love out, directing it specifically into the flame at the centre of the group, while visualizing total healing. Continue to direct healing energy for a few minutes.

▷ **6** Section 3: Give thanks for the healing received and channelled by each member of the group. Let the images slowly dissolve, breathe deeply and take your energy down into your feet to ground yourself, before opening your eyes and extinguishing the candle flame to end the meditation.

meeting your own soul

In this meditation, visualize yourself wearing soul robes of shimmering energies that both symbolize and veil the brightness of the spirit.

▷ **1** Get settled into a still and peaceful state, ready to visualize.

2 See yourself wrapped in your protective aura, which is firmly attached by a silver cord to the heaven (light) and earth (life) poles and suspended between them. This cord passes through your chakras within your aura.

3 Breathe in both light (from above) and life (from below) at the same time, so that they mingle as love. Breathe this out into your aura.

4 See yourself leaving your "mind space" and walking down into the area of your "heart space".

5 Settle reverently in front of the eternal flame that burns in a tiny lamp on a low table at the centre of your heart home. Gaze into this flame of love and enter a state of peace.

6 After a while look around your heart home and notice how it contains objects or images that remind you of those, alive or dead, with whom you share a bond. Love's bonds are eternal. Take comfort and support from this understanding.

7 Look down at yourself – you are wearing your soul robes of swirling energy. What colours do you see? They are your personal "energy signature".

8 You may finish your meditation at this point. Remember to give thanks for the healing of attitudes and relationships, and for any other help and guidance you have received. Look around you – your heart home will become adorned, as your loving relationships leave their impressions behind in the form of beautiful images. Let the images dissolve before grounding yourself thoroughly and possibly writing down your experiences. Alternatively, before finishing, you may wish to invite another soul (such as a beloved relative) to share your space before the eternal flame. They will appear quietly on a seat beside you and wait for you to become

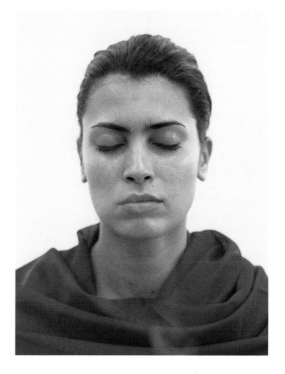

aware of their presence. Enjoy this meeting, thank them for responding and let their images dissolve before coming out of the meditation.

9 Once you have gained confidence you may wish to invoke a soul whose personality in this lifetime has been in conflict with your own, knowing that at soul level you share only love without any attempt to justify yourself or criticize another. It can be very helpful to "talk" about the attitudes and perceptions of your respective personalities. True souls are always in a state of peace. The ongoing healing effects upon both personalities can be truly amazing.

KARMA

The Eastern spiritual traditions assume that we all live a series of lives, gradually balancing out our negative and positive karma (the effect of our actions). The seeds of all past experiences lie buried deep in our souls. People we have interacted with before may be with us again now, as we evolve together through love and forgiveness, aided by meditation. Our actions in this life create the circumstances for our next incarnation, as we either take or ignore opportunities to release others from their negative karma through our unconditional forgiveness. By learning – often despite ourselves – to make choices dictated by love we spiral together toward the perfect freedom of existence (sat), consciousness (chit) and bliss (ananda) where life and light become one in love. It has been said that this freedom depends upon all of us for, since we are all one, there is ultimately only one of us to be liberated. This truth is becoming painfully obvious as regards the survival of our species and possibly even our planet.

▷ **Buddhist meditation follows the Buddha's own precept: "Look within, you are the Buddha."**

Glossary

ajna the brow chakra

anahata the heart chakra

ananda bliss

ananda maya kosha the soul body

anna maya kosha the physical body

asana a yoga posture

ashtanga Patanjali's eight limbs of yoga

bodymind an expression of the holistic relationship that exists between mental and physical processes

chakra a vortex at which energy channels meet in the subtle body; the seven main chakras are aligned with the spinal column

chit consciousness

dharana concentration on a single point or object

dharma the divine order

dhyana the state of meditation

ekagrata one-pointedness, focusing attention on a single object

granthi one of three knots of attachment that constrict the flow of energy through the nadis

guna one of the three inner properties of everything in nature

hatha yoga physical yoga practices designed to promote the flow of energy in the subtle body

japa repetition of a mantra, spoken or chanted, or repeated silently in the mind

karma the effect of past actions in this and previous lives

kosha one of the five levels of being

likhit japa the practice of repeatedly writing a mantra

mala a traditional string of 108 beads used to count the repetitions of a mantra

mandala a symbolic representation of the universe

manipura the navel chakra

mano maya kosha the instinctive mind

mantra a sacred sound that is repeated as a focus for meditation

mudra an attitude or gesture that reflects or generates a feeling or thought

muladhara the base chakra

nada the mystical sounds of inner vibrations, heard in meditation

nadi energy channel

niyama personal purificatory practices

OM the primordial sound, embodying the divine principle

plexus a concentration of nerve endings

prakriti nature, the changing substance of the material world

prana energy

prana maya kosha the energy body

pranayama breathing techniques used to achieve the meditative state

pratyahara the withdrawal of the senses from the external world

purusha spirit or consciousness, which is unchanging and eternal

raja yoga the "royal path" to meditation, the system of physical and mental practices expounded by Patanjali that lead to the state of expanded consciousness

rajas the guna of passion, desire and motion

sahasrara the crown chakra

samadhi the state of expanded consciousness that arises from the practice of meditation

samkhya a dualistic philosophy that asserts that creation is the result of the interaction of nature and consciousness

samyama the heightened state of consciousness engendered by dharana, dhyana and samadhi

sankalpa an affirmation

sat existence

sattva the guna of balance and harmony, required for meditation

svadisthana the sacral chakra

swadhyaya self-awareness

tamas the guna of intertia, ignorance and darkness

tapas self-discipline

Transcendental Meditation (TM) a meditation technique introduced by Maharishi Mahesh Yogi, based on the silent repetition of a personal mantra

tratak a meditative technique involving focusing the gaze on an object such as a lighted candle

Vedanta a Hindu spiritual tradition based on the teachings of the Vedas

Vedas the most ancient sacred texts of India

vijnana maya kosha the intellect

vishudhi the throat chakra

yama one of the five ethical precepts that form the foundation of yoga

yantra a diagrammatic representation of an abstract concept

"The spiritual journey is like a spiral path up and around a mountain, so that with each turn of the spiral you come back to the same point, only higher up and with a wider view."

Traditional wisdom

Index

Acknowledgements

The author and publishers would like to thank:
Our wonderful models, for their skill, cheerful patience and
willingness: Neil Casselle, Anna Ford, Patricia McLoughlin,
Antony Malvasi, Priya Rasanayagam and Nina
Zambakides. Our thanks also go to: Mariananda Azaz and
colleagues at the Self-Realization Meditation Healing
Centre, Yeovil, Somerset, UK, for the loan of their lovely
portable meditation stool; Meditation Designs, Totnes,
Devon, UK, for supplying us with a marvellous selection of
special meditation cushions and mats; Pat Coward for
compiling the index.

Extracts from The Yoga Sutras of Patanjali by Alistair Shearer
published by Rider. Used by permission of the Random
House Group Limited. For editions sold in the US and
Canada: Extracts appear from The Yoga Sutras of Patanjali by
Patanjali, translated by Alistair Shearer, copyright © 1982 by
Alistair Shearer. Used by permission of Bell Tower, a division
of Random House, Inc.

Thanks to the following agencies and individuals for
permission to reproduce their images:
t=top, b=bottom, r=right; l=left
p12t © Kevin R. Morris/Corbis; p12b © Araldo de
Luca/Corbis; p13tl © Bettmann/Corbis; p13r akg-
images/British Library; p13bl Don Last; p15tr and br Craig
Knowles; p16t National Museum of Karachi/Bridgeman
Art Library; p22 © The Purcell Team/Corbis; p41br Alistair
Hughes; p44t Fiona Pragoff; p59bl Don Last; p62r Peter
Anderson; p67b Don Last; p68b Stephen Brayne; p79b
Alistair Hughes; p87t Fiona Pragoff; p92t Fiona Pragoff